NAPOLEON, CEO

NAPOLEON, CEO

6 PRINCIPLES TO GUIDE & INSPIRE MODERN LEADERS

ALAN AXELROD

STERLING
New York

STERLING
New York

An Imprint of Sterling Publishing
387 Park Avenue South

ISBN 978-1-4027-7906-0 (Hardcover)
ISBN 978-1-4027-8893-2 (ebook)

Library of Congress Cataloging-in-Publication Data
Axelrod, Alan, 1952-
Napoleon, CEO : 6 principles to guide & inspire modern leaders / Alan Axelrod.
    p. cm.
Includes bibliographical references and index.
ISBN 978-1-4027-7906-0
1. Leadership. 2. Chief executive officers. 3. Napoleon I, Emperor of the French, 1769-
1821. I. Title.
HD57.7.A959 2011
658.4'092--dc22

2010051289

Distributed in Canada by Sterling Publishing
c/o Canadian Manda Group, 165 Dufferin Street
Toronto, Ontario, Canada M6K 3H6
Distributed in the United Kingdom by GMC Distribution Services
Castle Place, 166 High Street, Lewes, East Sussex, England BN7 1XU
Distributed in Australia by Capricorn Link (Australia) Pty. Ltd.
P.O. Box 704, Windsor, NSW 2756, Australia

For information about custom editions, special sales, and premium and
corporate purchases, please contact Sterling Special Sales at 800-805-5489 or
specialsales@sterlingpublishing.com.

Manufactured in the United States of America

2 4 6 8 10 9 7 5 3 1

FRONTISPIECE: Napoleon statue (1833) in the balcony of Les Invalides, Paris. France,
by Charles Émile Seurre. © Shutterstock/Jose Ignacio Soto

PICTURE CREDITS:
ii: © Shutterstock/Jose Ignacio Soto
v: Courtesy the Library of Congress Prints & Photographs Division / LC-DIG-ppmsc-05204
32, 60, 100, 142, 178, 222: From *The Life of Napoleon Bonaparte*, by W. H. Ireland,
London: John Cumberland, 1828.

For Anita and Ian

CONTENTS

Introduction

The Life of a Necessary Man

"Don't talk to me of goodness, of abstract justice, of natural law. Necessity is the highest law."

~Napoleon, during the "Hundred Days," April 1815

"He left France smaller than he found it, true; but you can't measure a nation like that. As far as France is concerned, he had to happen. It's rather like Versailles: it just had to be built. Don't let us haggle over greatness."

~President Charles de Gaulle, in conversation with his minister of culture, André Malraux, 1969

One hundred fourteen miles long and fifty-two miles wide, Corsica exploded into being through prehistoric volcanic eruptions in the Mediterranean Sea between Italy and France. Two-thirds of its roughly fourteen-hundred-square-mile area is rugged mountain country whose sharp contours reflect the violence of its geological birth. Napoleone di Buonaparte was born in the fiery island's principal town, Ajaccio, on August 15, 1769.

He was the second of the eight children born of attorney Carlo Maria Buonaparte and Maria Letizia Ramolino. Both parents were descended from minor Genoese nobility, who had settled in

Corsica—a possession of Genoa since 1347—during the sixteenth century. A dreary twenty-six-year revolutionary war began on the island in 1729, ending in 1755 with the founding of the Corsican Republic led by the charismatic nationalist Pasquale Paoli. Unable to drive the Genoese from the coastal cities even after the establishment of the republic, Paoli also proved unable to prevent Genoa from selling Corsica to France in 1764. Carlo Buonaparte became one of Paoli's lieutenants in what rapidly developed into a guerrilla resistance movement against French occupation, and the infant Napoleone was named after Carlo's brother, who was killed in this struggle.

Defeated in battle at Ponte Novu in 1769, Paoli fled to England, and Carlo Buonaparte made his own separate peace with the French, accepting appointment in 1777 as the Corsican representative to the court of King Louis XVI of France.

The turbulent politics of Corsica, with its passionate yet shifting allegiances, formed the background of Napoleone's childhood, as did the more ancient traditions of blood feud and vendetta, which were as deadly serious on Corsica as in Sicily. Yet in the foreground of his early life stood not his father, who was often absent, on duty in the French court, but his mother, who ruled over him, his elder brother, Joseph, and his younger brothers and sisters—Lucien, Elisa, Louis, Pauline, Caroline, and Jérôme—with an iron hand firmly placed in a tender velvet glove. He was thus the child of violent political, national, and quasi-tribal strife yet also the product of a strong mother, who was in equal parts formidable and loving.

Student and Cadet

Although Napoleone's early life unfolded on an island backwater steeped in conflict, he did reap the benefits of his family's local prominence and his father's French connections. Whereas most Corsicans were destined to lives of provincial obscurity and relative poverty, Napoleone was packed off to attend a private school in Autun, France, in January 1779. Raised speaking Corsican, he rapidly learned French and in May gained admission to one of France's twelve royal military academies, this one at Brienne-le-Château. His hastily acquired French was thick with the accents of his native island, and on this account, as well as for his dark Mediterranean complexion, he was teased mercilessly by the other cadets. Their taunts were intensified by his stubborn failure to be intimidated by them. The boy the others saw as a Corsican rube responded to abuse with the haughty disdain of Versailles royalty.

Doubtless, young Napoleone was lonely, but as he would do throughout his career, he converted adversity into opportunity. He used his isolation, which was both inflicted by others and self-imposed, to concentrate on study. His teachers noted his facility in history and geography, but they were most impressed by what seemed to border on genius in mathematics, especially geometry. Since geometry was vital to the art of navigation, he was advised to enter the navy. Those who counseled him assumed, of course, that he would join the French navy, but Napoleone knew that the British Royal Navy was preeminent in the world, and, feeling no particular allegiance to France, he seriously considered applying abroad. What stopped him was his admission, after completing the course of study at Brienne in 1784, to the École Militaire in Paris, the premier military college of France. Here he found another application for his geometrical mastery, the artillery service.

Carlo Buonaparte's death from stomach cancer in 1785 put the family in dire financial straits. Forced to cut short his studies at the École Militaire, Napoleone submitted himself to immediate examination by no less a figure than Pierre-Simon Laplace, eighteenth-century France's greatest mathematician, who certified his eligibility for graduation, even though he had completed but one year of the two-year program.

The Forge of Revolution

Napoleone di Buonaparte graduated in September 1785 with a commission as second lieutenant in an artillery regiment known as "La

Fère." He was assigned to the dull routine of garrison duty in Valence, Drôme, and Auxonne, but, with the eruption of the French Revolution in 1789, he departed on a leave of absence that would consume nearly two years.

Napoleone returned to Corsica, from where he wrote to Paoli in May 1789 of the "odious sight" of the French occupiers of the island who were "drowning the throne of liberty in waves of blood." While the Revolution raged on the French mainland, he presented himself as a Corsican nationalist yet threw his support behind the radical *French* Jacobins. He engineered his transfer from the regular French army to the post of adjutant in a volunteer Corsican militia battalion and gained promotion from second lieutenant to lieutenant colonel of the battalion by arranging the kidnapping of his opponents.

Lieutenant Colonel Buonaparte led his volunteers in a riot against a French army detachment in Ajaccio, and, when he ignored an order to rejoin regular army forces, he was summarily struck off the lists of the French army. This prompted him to return to Paris, where, instead of facing court martial, he boldly demanded not only readmission into the army but a promotion to captain of artillery. With the regular French army desperately in need of officers, both of his demands were met in July 1792.

The new captain also requested that he be allowed to return to Corsica to assist Paoli, who had ostensibly allied himself with the French revolutionary government. His commanding officers agreed, and Captain Buonaparte assumed co-command of a French assault on the Sardinian island of La Maddalena, only to discover that Paoli had turned against France, aligned with the English (who promised to support his bid for Corsican independence), and moved to sabotage the La Maddalena operation. This caused a dangerous rupture between Napoleone and Paoli, which prompted the entire Buonaparte family to take flight from Corsica to the French mainland in June 1793.

Hero of Toulon

Although Napoleone's Corsican sojourn had been turbulent and at times dangerous, it had also kept him out of the revolutionary bloodbath on the mainland. Shortly after he returned to Paris, he published in July 1793 *Le souper de Beaucaire* ("Supper at Beaucaire"), a Republican political and philosophical dialogue that, while not particularly original or distinguished as literature, struck a chord with the younger brother of the Jacobin leader Maximilien Robespierre, Augustin, who responded by securing Napoleone an appointment as commander of Republican artillery at the siege of Toulon (September 18–December 18, 1793) with the rank of major.

Toulon, on the southeastern French Mediterranean coast, was a counterrevolutionary stronghold that, occupied by British troops who were supported by a Royal Navy fleet riding at anchor in the harbor, had risen against the Republican government. Unchecked, the uprising could undo the French Revolution.

Exhibiting tactical mastery, charismatic command presence, and great personal courage, the young major executed a plan to take a hill overlooking Toulon's harbor, place his artillery there, and so threaten the British ships that they would have no choice but to evacuate, taking the occupying troops with them. Major Buonaparte personally led the assault on the hill, and although he was wounded in the thigh, he took his objective, deployed his guns, and, as he had intended to do, forced the British troops to depart, the Royal Navy to take flight, and the Royalist insurgents to surrender the city to the Republican government. For this, the twenty-four-year-old was catapulted to the rank of brigadier general and, on orders of the revolutionary Committee of Public Safety, awarded command of the artillery arm of the French Army of Italy.

A "Whiff of Grapeshot"

Soon after his victory at the Siege of Toulon, Napoleone di Buonaparte adopted the French spelling of his name, Napoleon Bonaparte, and dropped the particle "di" as savoring too strongly of the nobility. The victory had raised his star, but, in the universe of the French Revolution, stars often became shooting stars, bound for rapid extinguishment. When the anti-Jacobin "Thermidorian Reaction" of July 1794 overthrew the Robespierre brothers, Napoleon, perceived as their protégé, was placed under house arrest. His confinement lasted less than two weeks, but even after his release, he found himself out of favor.

In April 1795, he was transferred to the Army of the West, which was fighting the so-called War in the Vendée, a Royalist counterrevolution in the Vendée region of west central France. The new assignment was effectively a demotion, because he had been moved from the elite artillery to the common infantry. Unwilling to see his story written this way—he demanded a narrative arc of uninterrupted ascension—Napoleon claimed illness and thereby evaded having to accept the new posting. Instead, he was assigned to the Bureau of Topography of the Committee of Public Safety, an obscure position that cast him so far out of the inner circles of power that he briefly (and unsuccessfully) lobbied for transfer to Constantinople, from which he intended to offer his military services to the Ottoman Sultan in the hope of rising to power on the cusp of Europe and the Middle East.

Napoleon's dejection was intensified by the turbulent course of his engagement to the well-connected and quite beautiful Désirée Clary, whose sister Julie married his brother Joseph in 1794. He poured his heartache and frustration into a semiautobiographical romance titled *Clisson et Eugénie*. Failing to achieve catharsis, he hit bottom on September 15, 1795, when he was stricken from the list of regular army generals because of his refusal to serve in the Vendée.

Early the following month, on October 3, Parisian Royalists rose up against the National Convention, which had excluded them from the Directory, the new ruling body of the Republican government. Paul Barras, who had been among the leaders of the Thermidorian Reaction that had instigated Napoleon's house arrest, now proposed none other than Napoleon to command the defense of the Tuileries Palace, in which the National Convention had assembled and which the Royalists were threatening to attack and seize. Barras, it seems, was one prominent Parisian who had not forgotten Napoleon's brilliant triumph at Toulon.

Seizing the new opportunity, Napoleon decided on the unorthodox use of artillery to defend against a popular insurrection intent on overrunning the palace. He ordered the dashing young cavalryman Joachim Murat to capture a battery of heavy cannon, which Napoleon then deployed outside the Tuileries. On October 5, 1795–"13 Vendémiaire An IV" in the French Republican calendar–Napoleon opened fire on the insurrectionists, offering them (in the memorable understatement Thomas Carlyle used in his 1837 historical masterpiece, *The French Revolution*) a "whiff of grapeshot." In fact, Napoleon mowed down some fourteen hundred members of the mob, a stunning action that immediately dispersed them all and instantly ended the threat to the National Convention.

Almost as instantly, "13 Vendémiaire" publicly rehabilitated Napoleon Bonaparte, bringing down upon him a sudden cascade of fame, wealth, and power, all courtesy of the Directory that he had rescued. Promoted to Commander of the Interior, he was assigned full field command of the Army of Italy. Propelled by his newfound fame and fortune, Napoleon turned his back once and for all on Desirée and began an affair with the former inamorata of Paul Barras, the young widow Joséphine de Beauharnais. He married her on March 9, 1796.

It was almost certainly Barras who had instigated the marriage, and it was also he who urged the Directory to give Napoleon an important command. "Advance this man," he reportedly warned Directory leaders, "or he will advance himself without you."

On to Italy

Just two days after marrying Josephine, Napoleon left to assume command of the Army of Italy. While it was a major command, the

Army of Italy was also the smallest and least well supplied of the thirteen field armies of the French Republic. It may well have been that, in assigning Napoleon to this army, at least some members of the Directory hoped he would fail and, as a consequence, fade away.

But he did nothing of the kind. Napoleon instantly proved to be an inspiring commander, a thoroughly competent logistician, and a fine tactician, whose execution of tactics was brilliantly innovative. He compensated for his army's small numbers by incredibly rapid marches and deft maneuvers that allowed him to concentrate more of his force precisely in the places where the Austrians, substantially superior in strength overall, were at their weakest and most vulnerable. His early success culminated in the Battle of Lodi on May 10, 1796, in which he defeated the Austrians and drove them out of Lombardy.

An Austrian counterattack at Caldiero on November 12, 1796, inflicted a defeat on Napoleon, who, however, counter-counter-attacked at the Battle of Arcola (Battle of the Bridge of Arcole) during November 15–17, by which he was able to regain momentum and force the papal states into submission. At this point, radical atheists in the Directory urged Napoleon to invade Rome and dethrone the Pope. Although he had been baptized a Catholic in infancy, Napoleon neither revered nor feared the papacy, but he refused to act against the Pope on strategic grounds, reasoning that his removal would create a void that would only be exploited by the Kingdom of Naples and at the expense of the French position. The enemy, he reminded the Directory, was not the Pope, but Austria, and in March 1797 he advanced into that country and forcibly negotiated the Treaty of Leoben. Austria signed the treaty on April 17, 1797, ceding control of most of northern Italy and the Low Countries to France. Pursuant to a secret clause in the treaty that promised Austria the Venetian territories of Istria and Dalmatia, Napoleon invaded Venice, ending its eleven hundred years of independence and looting some of its extraordinary treasures. From Venice, as from everywhere he went in Italy, Napoleon sent wagonloads of riches back to the perpetually cash-strapped Directory. In this way, he won over the vast majority of doubters.

Militarily, Napoleon was a fairly conventional strategist. Even his tactics, though masterful, were hardly new. Throughout his life, he would claim to have learned everything from the commanders he called history's "Great Captains," who included Alexander the Great, Hannibal, and Julius Caesar among the ancients, and Prussia's Frederick the Great, Marshal Turenne of seventeenth-century France, and Sweden's seventeenth-century soldier-king Gustavus Adolphus among the moderns. Typically, he sought to envelop his enemy by making a small frontal attack designed to hold the main enemy force by the nose so that he could swing around with the bulk of his army to attack one or both flanks, or a flank and the rear. Although many generals of the late eighteenth century relied on simple brute-force frontal attacks, Napoleon's tactic, though more inventive, was not innovative, let alone radical. Unprecedented, however, were the skill, speed, ferocity, and tenacity with which he executed his attacks. Everything was mobile, even artillery, which he kept constantly on the move to support his infantry. No one had ever seen that before. Enemy commanders were left dazed, bewildered, intimidated, and even paralyzed by Napoleon's seemingly demonic movements.

Fruits of Victory

Napoleon's sweep through Italy netted 150,000 prisoners of war, 540 artillery pieces, and 170 regimental standards in the course of sixty-seven combat actions, which included eighteen important battles. Napoleon did not wait for final victory before promoting himself through two newspapers he authorized to be printed by the Army of Italy. These also circulated well beyond his forces, but to ensure that word of his fame spread—and was expressed in precisely the way he wanted—Napoleon added to his military newspapers *Le Journal de Bonaparte et des hommes vertueux,* a propagandistic periodical published in Paris beginning in May 1797.

After the elections of 1797 restored many Royalists to power, they foolishly condemned Napoleon's achievements in Italy and his bold diplomacy with Austria. This opposition gave Napoleon an excuse to dispatch to Paris one of his generals, Pierre Augereau, to instigate a coup d'état culminating in the purge of Royalists on September 4 (18 Fructidor in the Revolutionary calendar). Because the Royalists had taken sides against him, he was confident of the support of Barras and other Republicans of all stripes. In this way, Napoleon was catapulted to the top of the Republican power pyramid, and he was granted full authority to negotiate the Treaty of Campo Formio on October 17, 1797, which brought an end to the First Coalition of nations that had allied against the French revolutionary republic. The treaty both affirmed and added to the French gains made in the earlier Treaty of Leoben.

"Forty Centuries Look Down"

His Italian triumph had made Napoleon a hero among the people, and the Directors, jealous and fearful though many of them were, dared not oppose him. Yet Napoleon was hardly content to bask in the bright sunshine of his latest achievement. He understood the fleeting nature of fame, and no sooner had he returned to Paris than he began to look for the next great challenge.

The ultimate goal would be to definitively defeat Britain, an ancient rival of France that had taken on new menace since the Revolution. Although Napoleon began meeting with Charles Maurice de Talleyrand-Périgord, the wily and ruthless new French foreign minister, to plot an invasion of England, both men realized that French naval power was no match for the Royal Navy. Napoleon proposed holding the invasion in abeyance (many historians believe he never really intended to invade) and instead attacking Britain in a much less direct manner by seizing Egypt, which would immediately interdict English trade routes to India and position France favorably on India's doorstep. After establishing an alliance with the anti-British "Tiger of Mysore," Tipu Sultan, Napoleon intended to use Egypt as a base of operations for the invasion of India, from which he proposed to eject the English, landing upon the British Empire a political and economic blow from which it could never recover.

Talleyrand was on board with the Egyptian campaign, but the Directory was reluctant. Only Napoleon's immense popularity persuaded the Directors to approve the expedition. Besides, many of them felt that they could only benefit from Napoleon's absence from France.

From the beginning, Napoleon envisioned the Egyptian undertaking as far more than a military campaign. He wanted to introduce the Egyptians to the best that French civilization had to offer. After securing election to the French Academy of Sciences, he recruited 167 mathematicians, scientists, and educators to accompany the expedition. He intended the French conquest of Egypt to be, like the ancient conquests of Alexander, enlightened.

On June 9, 1798, the expedition reached Malta, at the time governed by the Knights Hospitaller, a noble order founded during the Crusades. Napoleon knew that those Knights who were of French origin had no love for their order's Grand Master, Ferdinand von Hompesch zu Bolheim, a Prussian, and so he did not hesitate to seize Malta, correctly surmising that no substantial resistance would be offered. Possession of the island gave Napoleon a key staging area and naval base for his Egyptian campaign.

Departing Malta, leaving behind only a modest garrison, Napoleon's expedition narrowly eluded a Royal Navy fleet under Admiral Lord Nelson. After landing at Alexandria on July 1, the French army fought the Mamelukes (soldiers of slave origin who had converted to Islam) at the Battle of Chobrakit on July 12, 1798. Once again, Napoleon showed himself to be a radically innovative master of artillery. After taking two Mameluke villages, he formed his army into defensive hollow squares and positioned artillery between each of the squares so that it could be brought to bear on the enemy no matter what side an attack came from. Thus the Mamelukes battered themselves fruitlessly against Napoleon's guns, losing large numbers with each attack they made.

Having discovered the poverty of Mameluke tactics at Chobrakit, Napoleon engaged them again at Embabeh, outside of Cairo, in the so-called Battle of the Pyramids, fought on July 21. "Soldiers," he famously exhorted his men, "from the summit of yonder pyramids, forty centuries look down upon you."

Although he was greatly outnumbered—20,000 versus 60,000—Napoleon once again resorted to defensive squares supported by mobile artillery and won a lopsided victory, in which 3,000 Mamelukes were killed or wounded, whereas French losses numbered just 29 dead and 260 wounded.

Despite his triumph on land, Napoleon's expedition suffered a terrible blow on August 1 at the Battle of the Nile, when Admiral Nelson finally caught up with the French fleet and destroyed or captured all but two of its ships, leaving the invasion force without seaborne support. Napoleon refused to bow to the defeat, however, and early in 1799 advanced from Egypt into Damascus (modern Syria and Galilee) with just 13,000 soldiers, who attacked and took in rapid succession the coastal towns of Arish, Gaza, Jaffa, and Haifa.

At this point, a new enemy presented itself: bubonic plague, the deadly effects of which were exacerbated by a shortage of supplies. After unsuccessfully attacking the fortress of Acre with his greatly weakened army, Napoleon turned back toward Egypt in May 1799. Overburdened with many sick troops, he ordered the poisoning of those languishing with plague, who (he reasoned—or rationalized) were doomed. On their return to Egypt, the depleted army fell under attack at Abukir on July 25, but Napoleon was able to beat back the Ottomans' amphibious invasion.

18 Brumaire

Information, Napoleon believed, was the most important commodity a commander could possess. Some members of the Directory had taken comfort in the popular general's distance from Paris, a circumstance they hoped would reduce what they considered his dangerously growing influence. But Napoleon ensured that he received a steady stream of newspapers and state dispatches no matter where he was campaigning. In this way, he learned of French reverses in a war with a new alliance of nations–the War of the Second Coalition–and, on his own authority, left for France on August 24, 1799. The Directory, outraged, threatened to punish Napoleon as a deserter, but, bankrupt and lacking popular support, it was powerless to act against him.

Opportunity now came to Napoleon from within the Directory itself. One of that body's members, Emmanuel-Joseph Sieyès, enlisted his support in the overthrow of the current government. A potent plot coalesced around Sieyès and Napoleon, which also included Napoleon's younger brother Lucien; politician Roger Ducos; Joseph Fouché, a Director later to become infamous as Napoleon's ruthless minister of police; and the formidable Talleyrand, who would be a central figure in Napoleonic government and whom Napoleon bluntly characterized–albeit almost admiringly–as "a piece of dung in a silk stocking."

On 18 Brumaire (November 9, 1799), Napoleon persuaded the Directors and other legislators to take refuge in the Château de Saint-Cloud, west of Paris, citing rumors of a dangerous Jacobin uprising brewing against them. On 19 Brumaire, Napoleon suddenly menaced the gathered legislators with troops, which left only those legislators who were in on the coup d'état in power at the Tuileries. They appointed Napoleon, Sieyès, and Ducos as "provisional consuls," invested with authority to govern at will.

Sieyès assumed that he would dominate the new triumvirate, but Napoleon outmaneuvered him with the same dazzling speed he employed in his military campaigns. He dashed off a new constitution–"Constitution of the Year VIII"–and managed to achieve election as "First Consul," essentially absolute dictator. Without hesitation, he took up residence in the palace of the beheaded Louis XVI, the Tuileries, from which he assumed the task of ruling France.

Against the Second Coalition

He did not remain there long. During the War of the Second Coalition, while Napoleon was occupied in Egypt, Austrian forces had reversed nearly all of the gains he had made in Italy and all but driven the French Army of Italy out of the country. Assuming personal command of that army, Napoleon led it across the Alps in 1800. After stumbling badly and nearly suffering total defeat at Genoa, he was able to mount a major counteroffensive at the Battle of Marengo (in Piedmont) on June 14, 1800. His hard-won victory was decisive, but his brother Joseph, to whom he delegated the task of negotiating terms with the Austrians, was unable to persuade them to recognize the French conquests in Italy. Napoleon accordingly ordered a renewal of hostilities and dispatched General Jean Victor Marie Moreau to attack the forces of Austria and Bavaria at Hohenlinden, east of Munich. Moreau's decisive victory moved Austria to sign the Treaty of Lunéville in February 1801, which not only affirmed but expanded French gains awarded in the Treaty of Campo Formio. The Treaty of Amiens, definitively concluded with Britain on March 25, 1802, and highly favorable to France, brought peace to Europe.

The peace, though general, proved short-lived, however. After the British reneged on their agreement to evacuate Malta and refused to accede to France's annexation of Piedmont as well as to Napoleon's "Act of Mediation" creating a new Swiss Confederation, Napoleon denounced Britain as "perfidious Albion." In May 1803, the British government declared war, and Napoleon responded by making new preparations to invade the British Isles.

Some modern historians regard these latest invasion preparations as, yet again, mostly an empty threat. Not only was the French navy still grossly inadequate to go up against the Royal Navy, French land forces were thinly spread and especially burdened by an effort to suppress the Haitian revolution, which threatened to unravel the entire French colonial empire. Slavery had been abolished in the French colonies as a result of the French Revolution, but, on May 20, 1802, Napoleon reestablished it, thereby triggering a slave revolt in the French West Indies. The Haitian nationalist leaders Toussaint Louverture and Jean-Jacques Dessalines enjoyed significant success in Haiti against French forces, which were badly depleted by yellow fever and other tropical diseases. France's New World possessions were becoming liabilities rather than assets, and Britain was clearly preparing to exploit France's growing vulnerability. Cash-strapped, Napoleon authorized Talleyrand—now his foreign minister—to divest France of its remaining possessions on the North American mainland (a region far too vast to be held against British attack). This resulted in the Louisiana Purchase, by which the government of President Thomas Jefferson paid $11,250,000 in cash (plus $3.7 million in canceled French debts to the United States) to acquire 524,800,000 acres of territory.

Napoleon the Reformer

From the start of his reign as First Consul through the period of his monarchy, Napoleon was alternately condemned as a tyrant and oppressor and hailed as a reformer and liberator. Both assessments have claims on validity. The leader who reinstated slavery into the French colonies also did much to improve the lives of French citizens.

He rationalized the routine activities of government and made them far more efficient and beneficial to the people. Under the French kings, government had rarely served the public. Under the Directory, it had served it poorly. Napoleon reformed the administration of most government departments, assigning clear central authority and making services more generally accessible and equitable. He instituted a schedule of heavy taxation, but also introduced reforms that made taxes relatively rational and fair. Under his administration, the government subsidized education, including higher education, and promoted scientific advancement. Napoleon began an ambitious program of public works, ranging from the construction of modern sewer systems to the improvement and expansion of the French road network. And he both defined and reformed the hitherto ambiguous and corrupt relationship between the Catholic Church and the French state by negotiating the Concordat of 1801 with Pope Pius VII.

Most celebrated of all Napoleon's civil reforms was his 1804 promulgation of the Code Civil, better known as the Code Napoléon, the creation of which, by legal experts, he closely supervised. The Code Civil was followed by new comprehensive sets of legislation and decrees governing criminal and commercial law. In sum, under Napoleon, the entire body of French law was subjected to revision and reform.

Having suffered the long oppression of kings, the bloody violence of the Reign of Terror, and the incompetence of government under the Directory, the French people generally appreciated life under First Consul Napoleon Bonaparte and approved the Constitution of the Year X (1802), the first article of which, "in the name of the French people," proclaimed Napoleon "First Consul for Life."

Napoleon the Emperor

If the French people supported—even adored—Napoleon, there was no end of factional plotting against his authority and even his life. "The bullet that will kill me is not yet cast," he declared on February 17, 1814, after a victory at the Battle of Montereau that halted the advance on Paris of a combined force of Austrians and Württembergers. The statement expressed an attitude that had long dominated his thinking, but this did not mean that he was passive in the face of conspiracies against him. When, in January 1804, his police minister Fouché uncovered an assassination plot involving the highly trusted General Jean Victor Marie Moreau, Napoleon acted on Talleyrand's counsel by ordering the abduction of Louis Antoine, Duke of Enghien, a relative of the French Bourbon kings. Charged with complicity in the plot, Enghien was subjected to a secret trial and executed on March 21, 1804. News of this judicial murder—for the charges were clearly unfounded—spread rapidly throughout the courts of Europe, which branded

Napoleon, for all his rhetoric of liberty and his gestures of reform, nothing more than a child of the Terror.

For his part, Napoleon exploited the 1804 plot to justify the next bold leap in his career. With his life obviously in continual danger, he argued, it was important for France that he establish a formal Bonapartist line of hereditary succession, which would preclude the restoration of the Bourbon kings and the undoing of the Revolution. In remarkably short order, a new constitution—the Constitution of the Year XII—established what it called the "First French Empire," with Napoleon elevated to Napoleon I, Emperor of the French. In effect, Napoleon had persuaded the people of France to agree that the only way to save the advances wrought by the French Revolution, including the ideals of the Republic, was to reverse the Revolution and end the Republic by reestablishing a hereditary monarchy.

Born in Corsican obscurity, Napoleon had made and remade himself several times. Now, on December 2, 1804, at Notre Dame Cathedral in Paris, he accepted the royal crown from the hands of Pope Pius VII and placed it on his head with his own hands. Then, taking another diadem from the Pope, he crowned Josephine his empress. A durable myth—that Napoleon, in a fit of impatience and an excess of arrogance, seized the crown from the Pope—sprang up around this coronation, but the proceeding had, in fact, been carefully choreographed in advance. Always mindful of symbolism, Napoleon wanted the people of France to see him as anointed by the pontiff, but he did not want to be seen as accepting the Pope as his overlord. The unconventional self-coronation was the result. On May 26, 1805, Napoleon crowned himself a second time, at Milan Cathedral, as King of Italy.

A New War

The very year that Napoleon made himself emperor and king, Britain, Austria, and Russia organized themselves as the core of a Third Coalition to oppose France. In response, Napoleon revived the idea of invading Britain, but a combined Spanish and French fleet suffered a tactical defeat at the Battle of Cape Finisterre off the coast of Galicia, Spain, on July 22, 1805, sending French Admiral Pierre Charles Silvestre de Villeneuve scurrying to safety in Cadiz. This effectively took the French navy out of action and forced Napoleon to shelve even the threat of invasion.

The world, however, was a big place, and Napoleon had more moves to make. In the Ulm campaign of September 25 to October 20, 1805, he led his army in a successful effort to envelop, contain, and defeat the Austrian forces poised to invade France. On October 20, 1805, Napoleon's Grande Armée took 30,000 prisoners at Ulm—a spectacular victory that was tempered by Lord Nelson's seaborne triumph at the Battle of Trafalgar the very next day. Not only did the British admiral decimate the French and Spanish fleets, he affirmed Britain's mastery of the seas for the remainder of the Napoleonic epoch and beyond (though at the expense of his own mortal wounding).

Trafalgar was but the latest in a series of French naval disasters, but Napoleon refused to let it stop his struggle against the Third Coalition. At the Battle of Austerlitz in Moravia on December 2, 1805, he defeated a numerically superior Russo-Austrian army in a horrific nine-hour fight. Napoleon held one tactical principle above all others: find the enemy's weak point and strike it before it can be strengthened. When he perceived weakness in the enemy's very center, he ordered an all-out attack, remarking, "One sharp blow, and the war is over."

It was. The overwhelming French victory at Austerlitz brought an end to the Third Coalition. By the Treaty of Pressburg (December 26, 1805), Austria ceded yet more territory, and the Holy Roman Empire, established in 962, ceased to exist when Francis II of Austria renounced the title of Holy Roman Emperor to become instead Francis I of Austria and "the Confederation of the Rhine," an entity created by Napoleon and consisting of portions of what are today Austria, the Czech Republic, Germany, Italy, Liechtenstein, and Poland. To ensure that Francis I would be forever his subject, Napoleon named himself "protector" of the confederation. Having now radically redrawn the map of Europe, Napoleon expressed his satisfaction with the achievement by commissioning the Arc de Triomphe on the Champs Élysées to commemorate the Austerlitz victory and all that it meant.

The War of the Fourth Coalition

Now that three European coalitions had borne down upon him, Napoleon once again turned from Europe to the Middle East in the hope of finding non-European allies. The Austerlitz triumph moved the Ottoman Sultan Selim III to recognize him as the emperor of France, which quickly led to an alliance against Russia and Britain.

Thus allied, Napoleon faced the Fourth Coalition that had now assembled to oppose France. On October 14, 1806, he led the French to victory against the combined forces of Prussia and Saxony at the Battle of Jena-Auerstädt, making the Kingdom of Prussia subject to the French Empire. This accomplished, he engaged a combined Russian and Prussian army at the Battle of Eylau in East Prussia during February 7–8, 1807. Outnumbered 67,000 to 43,000, Napoleon slugged it out with the enemy for fourteen hours. Both armies took virtually identical losses—as many as 15,000 killed, wounded, or captured on each side—but Napoleon had forced the enemy into retreat. Still, as his lieutenant Marshal Michel Ney mournfully observed, "What a massacre! And all for nothing."

On June 14, 1807, at the Battle of Friedland in Prussia, Napoleon more than recovered from the bloody draw at Eylau. With 70,000 men, he defeated a Russian army of 120,000, inflicting 30,000 casualties at the cost of 8,000 Frenchmen. The battle brought the Fourth Coalition to an end and resulted in two Treaties of Tilsit (July 7 and July 9, 1807), by which France (in a secret clause) sold out the Ottoman Empire (its ally) to Russia in return for French acquisition of the Dalmatian coast and the Ionian Islands. The second Tilsit treaty, with Prussia, forced that kingdom to cede all of its territory west of the Elbe River to a newly created Kingdom of Westphalia, which would be ruled by Jérôme Bonaparte, Napoleon's youngest brother. Having acquired control of a portion of Poland, Napoleon created the Duchy of Warsaw and placed King Frederick Augustus I of Saxony on its ducal throne, knowing that this monarch was firmly his to command.

By the first Treaty of Tilsit, the Russian czar also agreed to join in Napoleon's instrument of economic warfare against Britain, the Continental System. Put into place on November 21, 1806, the Continental System was an attempt to enlist all Europe into France's anti-English boycott. Although a bold experiment in economic warfare, it became Napoleon's greatest nonmilitary failure. The boycott did little if any damage to British trade, since, without control of the seas, Napoleon lacked the means of halting extensive British smuggling operations. The economic hardship it caused fell upon France, its empire, and its allies.

"The Spanish Ulcer"

Despite the failure of the Continental System, the French Empire, as of 1807, was coming remarkably close to fulfilling Napoleon's stated ambition of making "all the peoples of Europe one people and Paris the capital of the world."

In 1807, backed by Spain, Napoleon invaded Portugal. That nation had pointedly refused to comply with the Continental System, and the French emperor intended to teach it—and the rest of the world—a lesson. Yet even as he hoped to win support for his anti-English embargo, Napoleon proved himself a treacherous ally. He sent troops into Spain, ostensibly to reinforce the Franco-Spanish army already planted in Portugal. Instead, he mounted an invasion of Spain, imposing on an unwilling and resentful populace his brother Joseph as king in place of Charles IV. A popular uprising soon forced a French withdrawal from much of the country, where-upon Napoleon assumed personal command, defeated the Spanish army, and recaptured Madrid. When a British force arrived to support Spanish efforts to eject the French, Napoleon pushed it to the Spanish coast.

By January 1809, most of Spain had been pacified, but renewed aggression from Austria forced Napoleon once again to turn over command of his Spanish forces to his subordinates while he returned to France.

In his absence, the war—called the Peninsular War because it encompassed all of the Iberian Peninsula, both Portugal and Spain—went badly, especially after Arthur Wellesley, First Duke of Wellington, took over command of combined British and Portuguese forces. These, acting against the backdrop of debilitating guerrilla action, took a terrible toll on the 300,000 French troops Napoleon had left on the peninsula. "The Spanish ulcer," as he called the war, would drain French manpower until 1814, the year of his abdication. Reminiscing during his final exile on St. Helena after 1815, Napoleon would claim that all his "disasters [were] bound up in [the] fatal knot" that was the war on the Iberian Peninsula.

War of the Fifth Coalition

The Treaty of Pressburg—December 26, 1806—had made Austria and France allies. But it had never been a warm relationship, and in April 1809, the Austrian government broke the alliance and joined Britain, Sicily, Sardinia, and Tyrol in the Fifth Coalition. On receiving the news, Napoleon left Spain to take personal command of forces on the Danube and German fronts.

At first, he enjoyed his customary success, but, after faltering in crossing the Danube, the French army was defeated at the Battle of Aspern-Essling near Vienna, fought May 21–22, 1809. Although the Austrian archduke Charles drove the French back, he failed to capitalize on his victory in the way Napoleon himself surely would have. His reticence gave Napoleon time to rally and regroup for a new battle on July 5–6, at Wagram, east of Vienna. This time the French victory was so decisive that Austria signed the Treaty of Schönbrunn on October 14, 1809, ending the Fifth Coalition and forcing Austria to cede yet more territory and pay France a ruinous indemnity.

Although victory at Wagram had shattered the Fifth Coalition, Britain remained in the fight and sought to compel Napoleon to spread his forces thin by opening up a new front far from the others. The Walcheren campaign, which spanned July 30 to December 9, 1809, was intended to invade the continent via the Netherlands, providing relief to Austria while also destroying whatever remained of the French fleet, which was believed to have taken refuge in Flushing, an island port in the country's southwest.

The expedition was potentially a very good idea, but its logistics and execution were poor; many British soldiers were laid low by a sickness dubbed the Walcheren Fever, and delays were such that Napoleon was able to reinforce Antwerp, ultimately forcing the British out.

Not one to be confined to playing defense, Napoleon, in the midst of the action in Walcheren, invaded the papal states in 1808 and annexed them to France, citing the Pope's failure to support the Continental System. When an indignant Pius VII responded by excommunicating Napoleon, the emperor's officers in Italy took it upon themselves to abduct the pontiff. Not only did Napoleon refuse to disavow this action by ordering the Pope's release, he allowed the infirm man to be hauled from one part of the French Empire to another while his agents relentlessly but fruitlessly pressured the pontiff to agree to a new concordat with France. Even non–Roman Catholics were appalled at the French emperor's abuse of the Holy Father.

In 1810, with relations between Napoleon and the Catholic Church at an abysmal low, the emperor divorced Josephine (like Napoleon, serially unfaithful) and married the Austrian Marie Louise, Duchess of Parma. When thirteen French cardinals refused to attend the wedding ceremony, Napoleon had them clapped into prison. He did not dare imprison the Pope, but he did effectively enforce his five-year exile from Rome, which ended only with Napoleon's 1814 abdication.

War with Russia

Napoleon and Czar Alexander I of Russia had maintained cordial relations since the Treaty of Tilsit in 1807. Over the years, however, the Russian nobility chafed under the Napoleonic yoke and urged the czar to end the alliance with France. Alexander I resisted the pressure, but in 1811 sought finally to placate the nobles by defying Napoleon to the extent of easing restrictions imposed by the operation of the Continental System in Russia. This led to Napoleonic saber rattling, which, in turn, prompted Alexander to begin preparations for a possible offensive against the French Empire with the objective of retaking (for Russia) Polish territory controlled by France.

Although Alexander's preparations were ostensibly secret, Napoleon's network of spies was extensive and sophisticated. In response to the intelligence he was receiving about Russian mobilization, Napoleon embarked on an extraordinary expansion of his Grande Armée, to nearly half a million men. His intention was to invade Russia preemptively, before Alexander could launch an invasion of the French Empire. In this, Napoleon committed two grave errors. His first was neglecting quality in favor of quantity. Hitherto, his most successful campaigns had been mounted by relatively small armies—usually smaller than those he fought against—but always manned by highly trained and thoroughly committed troops under the command of superb officers. Except for the superb veterans of the Imperial Guard, the army he brought to Russia was indifferently manned and was, in any case, unwieldy. Its vast numbers were more liability than asset—especially in the vast wastes of Russia. And that was the emperor's second terrible mistake. He ignored warnings that Russia's very size, combined with a harsh climate and poorly developed infrastructure, was capable of swallowing armies whole.

He began the invasion on June 23, 1812. Although he hoped to recruit Polish allies for the expedition—and therefore dubbed his campaign the "Second Polish War"—he refused to give the Polish nationalists what they wanted: leave to create an independent Poland out of the Duchy of Warsaw and any formerly Polish territory recaptured from Russia. Thus, from the outset, Napoleon sacrificed valuable support.

That was the first great frustration of the campaign. The next was the refusal of the Russians to engage in anything like a decisive battle. The Russian strategy was largely one of retreat and avoidance of major battle followed by more retreat. In this way, the French army was drawn deeper and deeper into the Russian interior. What few battles developed ended in Russian defeat, but never decisively so, and the deeper the French army ventured, the less its soldiers found. The Russian army was destroying crops and anything else of value in the ruthless execution of a scorched earth policy. Napoleon had always insisted that his soldiers live off the land. Now he had an oversized army but lacked the means to feed either men or horses. French losses from privation, starvation, disease, and desertion were far more staggering than any mere battle could produce. By the time Napoleon reached the outskirts of Moscow on September 7, 1812, he had no more than 130,000 "effectives" under his command—somewhat more than 20 percent of the number with which he had begun the campaign.

On September 7, the Russian army finally took a stand at the Battle of Borodino. Measured by casualties, the battle—the bloodiest single day of the Russian campaign—was a terrible Russian defeat: of 120,000 men engaged, as many as 45,000 were killed, wounded, or captured, while French losses numbered perhaps 35,000 killed, wounded, or captured out of 130,000 engaged. Yet Napoleon and his battered army were simply too exhausted to pursue the Russians after they had been routed. Had they done so, the Russian army would have ceased to exist. As Napoleon later expressed it, at Borodino, the "French showed themselves to be worthy of victory, but the Russians showed themselves worthy of being invincible."

The retreat of the Russian army admitted the French forces into Moscow without further resistance. Napoleon's assumption was that, with the fall of his capital, Alexander I would seek surrender terms. Instead, the czar ordered the city to be burned. Much of it was, and what remained was stripped and deserted by its inhabitants. Napoleon had won an empty shell.

In rage, frustration, and heartbreak, Napoleon and his surviving troops lingered in and about the ghost city for a month before beginning the long march back to France. By this time, the Russian winter was already starting to take hold. Men starved. Men froze. In November, a brutal crossing of the frozen Berezina River (in modern Belarus) reduced the French army to roughly 40,000 men, less than 10 percent of its original strength. From that time to this, "Berezina" has served the French as a synonym for *catastrophe*.

War of the Sixth Coalition

It is an extraordinary testament to Napoleon's hold over the French people that he survived the Russian catastrophe and continued to occupy the throne. The Russian nightmare left him unchastened, and he rapidly rebuilt his army to a field strength of 350,000 by 1813. But the rest of Europe took note of Napoleon's defeat, and Prussia, Austria, Sweden, Great Britain, Spain, and Portugal joined Russia to form the Sixth Coalition.

Napoleon met the new alliance aggressively, dealing out a series of defeats in Germany, the most consequential of which came at the Battle of Dresden on August 26–27, 1813. Napoleon stunned the Austrian general, Karl Philipp Fürst zu Schwarzenberg, by defeating his 214,000-man army (Austrian, Prussian, and Russian) with an army of little more than half its size—135,000 men. Days later, however, at the Battle of Kulm, in Bohemia, on August 29–30, a French force of 32,000, commanded by Dominque Vandamme, Laurent Gouvion Saint-Cyr, and Auguste-Frédéric-Louis Marmont, was defeated by a substantially larger Coalition force. This paled in comparison to what happened at the Battle of Leipzig during October 16–19, when Napoleon's 195,000-man army was overwhelmed by 430,000 Coalition troops. It was the biggest battle of the Napoleonic Wars and, indeed, the biggest European battle before World War I. French losses were 58,000 killed, wounded, or captured; the Coalition lost 54,000 killed or wounded.

The End—Almost

The Battle of Leipzig sent Napoleon falling back on France, his army having been reduced to no more than 70,000 effectives, with perhaps another 40,000 troops in marginal condition. Dogging him throughout the retreat was a Coalition army of at least 300,000, which attacked from virtually all directions. Despite some victories, Napoleon was unable to prevent the fall of Paris to the troops of the Coalition in March 1814.

Unwilling to concede defeat, Napoleon announced his intention to march to retake Paris. In response to this proposal, Marshal Ney led some of his fellow marshals in a mutiny on April 4, 1814. With defiant confidence, Napoleon insisted that the army would *follow him,* not the marshals. When Ney disputed this, Napoleon folded, abdicating the throne in favor of his son. The Allies of the Sixth Coalition believed they held all the cards and rejected any conditional abdication. Napoleon had no choice but to abdicate unconditionally on April 11, 1814.

The Coalition members ordered Napoleon's exile to the Mediterranean island of Elba, about twelve and a half miles off the coast of Tuscany. He was permitted to retain the title of emperor; but his empire now consisted of the twelve thousand men, women, and children who lived on the island. His wife and son took up separate residence in Vienna.

Prior to the retreat from Moscow, Napoleon had acquired a poison pill, intending to commit suicide rather than endure capture by the Russians. Before departing for Elba, he swallowed that pill, which, however, proved ineffective. Napoleon not only survived but went on to rule Elba much as an emperor would rule any empire. He assembled a tiny army and navy, and he decreed to the inhabitants of his domain certain principles of modern agriculture.

Mostly, however, Napoleon stewed impatiently in captivity. At length, fearing that Elba was but a stop on the way to a more remote exile, he somehow managed to elude the ever-present guards and, on February 26, 1815, escaped from the island, landing at Golfe-Juan, France, on the twenty-eighth.

The Bourbon Royalists who now controlled the government ordered the 5th Regiment to apprehend and arrest Napoleon. The troops found him near Grenoble on March 7. In an extraordinary moment of history, Napoleon cantered up to the column of soldiers, dismounted, and walked toward them.

"Here I am," he called out. "Kill your Emperor, if you wish."

In one voice, the soldiers of the 5th called out "Vive L'Empereur!"

Instead of arresting Napoleon, they marched with him to Paris. Word outran the march, and a terrified Louis XVIII fled. On March 13, the European leaders meeting to decide the fate of post-Napoleonic Europe proclaimed Napoleon an outlaw. On March 17, a new coalition of Great Britain, the Netherlands, Russia, Austria, and Prussia pledged to field an army of 150,000 to recapture Napoleon and end his reign once and for all.

A Hundred Days to Waterloo

On March 20, 1815, Napoleon arrived in Paris and, the Bourbons having decamped, resumed governing. After little more than two months, he had assembled a loyal army of 200,000. Never one to await the development of circumstances to which he must respond, Napoleon resolved to act first and thereby create his own history.

He would take aggressive offensive action to prevent the union of approaching British and Prussian armies by attacking between them. The battlefield would be in and around Waterloo, in what is today Belgium but was at the time part of the United Kingdom of the Netherlands.

What historians call the Waterloo campaign began on June 16, with the culminating battle commencing on Sunday, the eighteenth. Napoleon had 72,000 men available against 118,000 of the Seventh Coalition (Britain, Prussia, United Netherlands, Hanover, Nassau, and Brunswick), led by the Duke of Wellington and the Prussian field marshal Gebhard Leberecht von Blücher. Both were formidable opponents, Wellington celebrated as the "Iron Duke" and Blücher as "Marschall Vorwärts"—*Marshal Forward*—on account of his aggressive fighting style. Wellington had direct command of the Anglo-Dutch forces, Blücher of the Prussian and associated German forces. In essence, then, Napoleon led his single outnumbered army against two full opposing armies. He advanced from the south as Wellington closed in from the northwest and Blücher from the east. No other commander would have stood a chance in such circumstances and against such opponents, but as the always-blunt Wellington put it after the battle, the Waterloo campaign was "a damned serious business . . . the nearest-run thing you ever saw in your life."

Napoleon was relentless in his attacks against Wellington's army, which arrived on the field before Blücher could get into full engagement. Always looking to exploit weakness and aware that the expiration date of such an opportunity was always imminent, Napoleon was determined to drive Wellington from the field, which he did at a crossroads called Quatre-Bras, just south of Waterloo, on June 16. But despite withdrawing, Wellington's forces remained intact and coordinated, and while Napoleon concentrated against Wellington, Blücher arrived in force at Wavre and, to the west, at Waterloo. Although the Wavre fight, like that at Quatre-Bras, went to the French, the French collapse at Waterloo was total, as Napoleon's right, left, and center all crumbled in an end so decisive that the very word *Waterloo* has become a synonym for any fatal, final failure.

Routed, the remnants of the French army—about 24,000 men—melted from the field like so much snow in spring as the forces of the Seventh Coalition advanced into France to restore Louis XVIII to the throne. Napoleon pondered taking flight to the United States, to find refuge in French New Orleans, but instead, on July 15, he gave himself up to Captain Frederick Maitland, skipper of the Royal Navy's HMS *Bellerophon,* and demanded political asylum. He had been emperor of the French, after his escape from Elba, for just one hundred days.

Exile

The Desolator desolate!
The Victor overthrown!
The Arbiter of others' fate
A Suppliant for his own!

~Lord Byron, "Ode to Napoleon Buonaparte," 1814

Napoleon was exiled a second time, but to a place as remote as any in the world: the island of St. Helena, at the time a British posses- sion, located in the Atlantic Ocean some twelve hundred miles from any other substantial body of land. He was settled first in part of an English estate, The Briars, but was soon moved to the more austere Longwood House, a somewhat tumbledown grand manor occu- pying an inhospitable site perpetually lashed by cold, damp winds. Some believed that Napoleon's British keepers lodged him there with the express purpose of undermining his health. For his part, Napoleon persevered, surrounded by a small band of devoted fol- lowers as he dictated his memoirs.

The world did not forget him. Escape plots were hatched in South America, the United States, and elsewhere. They came to nothing, and the months passed into years. By early 1821, his health was declining rapidly. His father, Carlo Maria Buonaparte, had died of stomach cancer, and Napoleon had long suffered from digestive and stomach ailments. He seemed now to be succumbing to them.

By May 3, Napoleon's physician, Dr. Francesco Antommarchi, announced that he could do nothing more than try to make his patient comfortable as the inevitable approached. On May 5, Father

Ange Vignali was summoned to hear Napoleon's confession and administer last rites. Those present at the deathwatch heard the exile gasp out a four-item list: "France, *armée, tête d'armée*, Josephine" ("France, army, head of the army, Josephine"). They were the last words of a man who had been born on a small island and died on one even smaller, yet who, between that birth and that death, reshaped much of the world and redirected all of the history that followed him.

1

Audacity
and
Character

Lesson 1
Establish Credibility

> "I made the troops fire ball [live ammunition] at first because to a
> mob who are ignorant of firearms, it is the worst possible policy to
> start out by firing blanks. For the populace, hearing a great noise,
> are a little frightened after the first discharge, but, looking around
> them and seeing nobody killed or wounded, they pluck up their
> spirits, begin immediately to despise you, become twice as inso-
> lent, and rush on fearlessly, and it becomes necessary to kill ten
> times the number that would have been killed if ball had been
> used in the first place."
>
> ~Napoleon in exile at St. Helena, quoted in
> Felix Markham, *Napoleon*, 1963

In Paris, on October 3, 1795, Royalists rebelled against the revolutionary National Convention because of their exclusion from the
Directory, the newly created French government. Napoleon was
given command of a military force hurriedly cobbled together to
defend the Convention at the Tuileries Palace. On October 5,
Napoleon ordered Joachim Murat, a young cavalry officer destined to become one of the marshals of Napoleonic France, to
commandeer some artillery and direct the cannon against the mob.
While Thomas Carlyle wrote that Napoleon offered the attackers
a "whiff of grapeshot," it was, in fact, a full-on artillery assault with
live ammunition that mowed down some fourteen hundred Royalists, summarily ending the rebellion and elevating Napoleon to
great prominence.

As he related at the end of his career, while in his final exile
at St. Helena, Napoleon refused to deal in empty threats and
instead established credibility with a vigorous application of

[33]

violence, arguing that, in the long run, such a demonstration actually saved lives.

> **Nothing erodes credibility** more thoroughly than empty threats or empty promises. Words are important in leadership, but that cliché about action speaking louder than words is a cliché precisely because it conveys much truth. An action, especially one that is sufficiently large as to be audacious, is an investment. It is proof that you have, in a phrase Warren Buffett has often used, skin in the game. It is a declaration of confidence and an embrace of risk. It is a claim on credibility.

■

Lesson 2
Make Yourself Famous

> "In Paris, nothing is remembered for long. If I remain doing nothing for long, I am lost."
> ~ Napoleon, quoted in Felix Markham, *Napoleon*, 1963

After the success of the first Italian campaign (1796–97), Napoleon worried that the balance of his career would sink into anticlimatic obscurity, and so he immediately began to plan his next campaign—this one in Egypt.

For Napoleon, fame was the door to power, and only through spectacular achievement could he hope to win fame, which would give him the power to achieve more and thereby build greater and greater fame. Never an end in itself for Napoleon, fame served to fuel further conquest.

Some people thrive on fame for its own sake. Others shun the limelight. If the latter describes you, think of fame not as an end in itself but a means of building a leadership career. To lead any organization effectively, you must make yourself famous, even if only within the organization. Fame is built on achievement, provided that the achievement is perceived as bringing benefit to the enterprise. Associate yourself with positive change, the bolder and more beneficial the better.

■

Lesson 3
Take Ownership

> "Every commander responsible for executing a plan that he considers bad or disastrous is criminal: he must point out the flaws, insist that it be changed, and at last resort resign rather than be the instrument of the destruction of his own men."
>
> ~ "Observations on the Campaigns of 1796 and 1797,"
> quoted in Jay Luvaas, *Napoleon on the Art of War*, 1999

With great power comes grave accountability. For Napoleon, the claim that you were "only following orders" was no excuse for failure. A commander, he asserted, is not shielded from responsibility "by an order from a minister or a prince who is absent from the theater of operations." It is, Napoleon declared, the solemn responsibility of the commander in the field to take ownership of all actions and their probable result. Although he believed that an unbroken chain of command was vital to good military order, the conscience and informed judgment of the commander at the front trumped remotely issued orders when those orders were likely to result in something "bad or disastrous." Knowingly executing bad orders was, in his view, criminal, as was engaging in a battle that the commander was convinced he would lose.

Early in his career, as a field commander, Napoleon demanded great autonomy and accepted full responsibility for the consequences of that autonomy. Later, as supreme commander and emperor, he entrusted his top field marshals with the same autonomy he had earlier demanded for himself. He was convinced that only the general closest to the dynamic realities of a battle could make intelligent decisions governing the execution of strategic orders.

Responsibility is always more valuable than obedience. The notion that the top managers can see the big picture whereas the vision of subordinate managers is more or less restricted to the situation for which they are directly responsible is based on assumptions made during an era in which corporate structures were universally hierarchical. Today, in most organizations, these assumptions are obsolescent if not obsolete. Most organizations make more information available to more levels of management, so that more managers have access to the big picture. Instead of asserting the sanctity of a chain of command above all else, it is a far more effective leadership policy to require all managers to take ownership of their decisions, to refuse to excuse a bad decision on the grounds that it was the result of orders from on high, and to require the manager who executes a plan to evaluate the plan and to object to it if she believes it flawed.

■

Lesson 4
Do an Arcola

> "After watching several futile and costly assaults . . . Napoleon
> jumped from his horse, pulled together some troops by appealing
> to 'the conquerors of Lodi bridge,' wrapped a flag around a sword
> and started toward the [Bridge of Arcole]."
>
> ~Robert Asprey, *The Rise of Napoleon Bonaparte*, 2000

"Never has a field of battle been as disputed as that of Arcola," Napoleon wrote to his chief benefactor on the Directory, Lazare Carnot, on November 19, 1798. The Battle of Arcola (or Bridge of Arcole), which spanned November 15–17 during the first Italian campaign, was Napoleon's audacious bid to cut off the line of operation of the numerically superior Austrian army of General József Alvinczi.

Losses on both sides were high as a result of the Battle of Arcola, and Napoleon failed to destroy Alvinczi's army, which managed to withdraw intact. Although he did prevent the Austrians from capturing the important Italian city of Mantua, he failed to take the Arcole bridge, and, tactically considered, the battle itself probably should be counted a Pyrrhic victory for Napoleon—significantly more costly than it was worth.

Absent the general's heroic gesture with sword and flag, the battle would surely have been written off as futile. Instead, it became the context of a moment immediately enshrined in popular Napoleonic lore and depicted in a number of paintings, including an 1801 canvas by Antoine-Jean Gros (1771–1835) that shows a youthful, handsome, long-haired Bonaparte calmly advancing as he casts a steely glance back toward his troops. Despite its title, *Bonaparte at the Bridge of Arcole* includes nothing of the bridge or, for that matter, of the men Napoleon led. Its subject is exclusively Bonaparte, and it became one of the most famous of the many portraits of him. The cost and the questionable military value of the victory mattered far less than the image Napoleon had created at Arcole. It would carry him far.

Grand gestures and bold statements are inherently risky. Pitching a big prospect, you present a proposal designed to bowl him over, and he yawns. At the Arcole bridge, Napoleon risked far more—namely, his very life. He did so, in part, because he glimpsed the possibility of a great victory, a long shot, to be sure, but a possibility. More urgently, however, he saw the imminent probability of a lost opportunity or even a defeat if he did not do something audacious. Militarily, he and his army would have survived without his gesture, but the perception of Napoleon as a virtually invincible general would have suffered. It was as much to prevent this—and thereby to control popular perception—than to achieve an unlikely victory that Napoleon risked his life by wrapping the flag around his sword and leading the advance.

In so much that we do, it is perception that counts or at least counts most. Sometimes it actually makes sense to risk all on a single bold gesture.

■

Lesson 5
The Resolution to Conquer

> "In war tentative measures . . . lose everything."
> ~ Quoted in Jay Luvaas, *Napoleon on the Art of War*, 1999

What Napoleon described as "firmness of character and the resolution to conquer at any price" was the quality that separated a winning general from a commander who courted defeat by his willingness to hedge bets with "tentative measures." Napoleon saw victory versus defeat as binary. Either a leader resolved "to conquer at any price," or he settled for "tentative measures" and thereby set himself up to lose. No middle ground was possible.

> **Failure to commit** fully to victory is a de facto commitment to defeat.

■

Lesson 6
Believe Your Own Story

> "I am destined to change the face of the world; at any rate this is my belief."
>
> ~ To Joseph Bonaparte in 1804, quoted in Felix Markham,
> *Napoleon*, 1963

Writers on Napoleon frequently quote the first part of his 1804 remark to his brother, Joseph, yet rarely add the second part, which speaks volumes about his character.

"I am destined to change the face of the world" is an audacious presumption of fact. Add "at any rate this is my belief," however, and the statement becomes a sober self-perception and far less presumptuous, suggesting nothing more than that Napoleon built his identity and career according to a self-narrative in which (as he was apparently well aware) he *chose* to believe. Delusion? No. Napoleon's self-perception was largely self-calculated.

> **Script your career.** Write yourself a role, but be sure to make it a good one. Then act it convincingly. Choose to *believe* in your personal drama, and you will make the part totally convincing to others.

■

Lesson 7
Serve

> "I fear insurrection caused by a shortage of bread—more than a
> battle against 200,000 men."
>
> ~Quoted in Felix Markham, *Napoleon*, 1963

In 1970, philosopher-consultant Robert K. Greenleaf published an essay titled "The Servant as Leader," in which he coined the phrase "servant leadership," thereby effectively launching what many call today the "servant leadership" movement. It is founded on the idea of leading an organization by giving top priority not to yourself and your personal advancement or even to the advancement of your business, but to providing benefit to your colleagues and clients, whose servant you are.

Few writers on leadership today would characterize Napoleon as a servant leader. He did, after all, come to power through conquest and, having attained power, crowned himself emperor. Yet Napoleon himself saw himself first and foremost as a servant. He considered it his primary mission to serve those he led lest he lose his right to lead—if not his life as well.

Although Napoleon believed his greatest service to his countrymen and, perhaps, to humanity itself was the "Napoleonic code," the massive body of enlightened civil law he promulgated for France in 1804, he did not see himself as a servant in any philanthropic sense. He was instead a servant by grim necessity who understood and accepted the bargain into which he had entered: fail to deliver satisfaction, especially on the most basic of levels, and he would be overthrown.

Even Napoleon—conqueror, looter, self-crowned emperor—knew that a leader's most important function was to serve those he led. Fail in this, and you fail your enterprise. Fail in this, and you forfeit leadership. For it is not an employment contract or a job title that sustains you as a leader, but the daily permission, concession, and support of those you serve.

Lesson 8

Time Your Audacity

"The art of being sometimes audacious and sometimes very prudent
is the secret of success."

~Letter to Joseph Bonaparte, July 30, 1806

Napoleon put a premium on bold action, decisiveness, and innovation—qualities he summed up with the word *audacity*. Yet he was also capable of telling his youngest brother, Jérôme, that one did not "require spirit in war, but exactitude, character, and simplicity." This outlook need not, however, be viewed as conflicting with audacity. A successful general, according to Napoleon, knew when to be prudent and when to be audacious.

Napoleon considered Frederick the Great, Caesar, Turenne, and other "Great Captains" to be more consistently audacious than he himself was. They were successful more often than not, whereas his own Marshal Joachim Murat, whom he professed to love "because of his brilliant bravery," also "always committed stupid mistakes." Although Napoleon asserted that Murat understood how to conduct a campaign better than his most celebrated marshal, Michel Ney, he was still a "poor general." The reason was that he was not master of the "art of being sometimes audacious and sometimes very prudent." Instead, he was always audacious, even waging war on the fly, without maps.

Audacity for Napoleon was of greatest value in the execution of a well-thought-out plan. The plan itself required prudence. "One must be slow in deliberation and quick in execution," Napoleon wrote to his stepson, Eugène de Beauharnais—Prince Eugène—on August 21, 1806. Moreover, once the plan has been executed audaciously, the follow-up must be prudent. "To win is not enough," he counseled brother Joseph on November 10, 1808, "it is necessary to profit from success." And that required prudent planning.

Value audacity, but do not abandon prudence. Lavish deliberate caution on creating a plan that can be executed swiftly. The place of prudence is in preparation and follow-through. The moment for audacity is the moment of execution. The hard questions associated with doubt and even self-doubt are actually of great value when creating a plan. They must, however, yield to audacity when the plan is put into action.

■

Lesson 9
Leadership Onstage

"It is essential to display confidence."
~Letter to Eugène de Beauharnais, Prince Eugène, April 30, 1809

A general, Napoleon believed, was an actor and had but one role to play: that of the confident leader. He did not require a general to be confident or to feel confident. He did require a consistent display of confidence; whether it was counterfeit or genuine was immaterial.

In any organization, attitude, demeanor, and sentiment trickle down from the top. They do not rise up from the bottom. If the boss displays confidence, her enterprise will be confident, and its actions will be the products of confidence. To the degree that the boss falters in this display, the enterprise will lose its confidence. There is no excuse for failing to display confidence. The display need have nothing to do with the reality either of circumstances or feelings. The most elementary acting is all that's required. If you need motivation for your role, just remember that all of an organization's emotional cues are taken from the top.

Lesson 10
Enforce Ethical Standards

> "Every straggler who . . . detaches himself from his unit to maraud
> will be arrested, judged by a military commission, and executed
> within the hour."
>
> ~Order of the Day, May 14, 1809

Napoleon typically sought voluntary cooperation from the people of territories he conquered and occupied. Under some circumstances, the terms of occupation were harsh and even violent; however, whenever and wherever possible, Napoleon chose to emulate such conquerors as Alexander the Great and Caesar, who generally brought order, justice, and other benefits to territory they occupied, so that, often, they were popularly regarded as liberators rather than conquerors.

Eliciting voluntary cooperation required establishing relations based on trust and fair treatment between the occupying army and the conquered people. Accordingly, Napoleon required good behavior from officers as well as enlisted soldiers and specifically forbade looting, stealing, marauding, and other unlawful acts against civilian populations. To enforce these prohibitions, he ordered (on May 14, 1809) all violators to be arrested, tried, and (if guilty) executed within an hour of the trial verdict. (In a later campaign, in 1812, Napoleon extended the time between a guilty verdict and execution to a more leisurely twenty-four hours.)

The members of an organization will take ethical standards seriously only if management treats them seriously.

Ensure that the ethical standards of your organization are published clearly, fully, and unambiguously. All violations of or questions relating to ethical standards must be addressed fully, in writing, and promptly. It is a mistake to rush to judgment, but, in the case of any alleged violation, the process of investigation must begin without delay.

Lesson 11
Higher Education

> "Knowledge of the higher parts of war is acquired only through the study of history of the wars and battles of the Great Captains, and from experience. There are no precise or fixed rules."
>
> ~Letter to General Henri-Jacques-Guillaume Clarke,
> October 1, 1809

Tactics, engineering, the elements of artillery, and the like, Napoleon said, "can be learned in treatises, much like geometry," but what he called the "higher parts" of war could be acquired (in the absence of actual and extensive experience) only by studying those commanders he deemed history's "Great Captains"—Alexander the Great, Hannibal, and Julius Caesar among the ancients, Prussia's Frederick the Great, Marshal Turenne of seventeenth-century France, and Sweden's seventeenth-century soldier-king Gustavus Adolphus among the moderns. They shared a facility for exercising prodigious imagination through reason and yet were always driven by audacity. Their movements were rapid, decisive, and precise.

No hard and fast lessons come from the higher education history and experience provide. But, for the attentive student, history and experience do offer an abundance of inspiration, which, in real-world situations, is far more valuable than "precise or fixed rules." Inspiration is flexible, agile, and adaptable and, therefore, far better suited to the dynamic, living, fluid reality of war than are inflexible, hard, and brittle rules.

Some people purposely break the rules. Others—the true leaders—understand that it is life itself that breaks the rules. Hard and fast rules are brittle and bound to be broken. Unlike rules, which are by definition dead, the living lessons of hard-won achievement, successful precedent, and triumph in adversity are flexible enough to enable mastery of live situations unfolding in real time. *Memorize* the rules, but *study* these lessons.

Lesson 12
Think Beyond the Usual Categories

"Fortified towns are useful for defensive as well as offensive war."
~ "Notes on the Art of War," quoted in Jay Luvaas,
Napoleon on the Art of War, 1999

Nothing is more absolute in theoretical discussions about the nature of war than the distinction between defense and offense. Napoleon possessed the genius of thinking beyond even this universally accepted dichotomy.

No commander would question that the function of a fortified town is to defend against invasion. By definition, a fortification is stationary, and, therefore, also by definition, it should play no offensive role, since offense implies mobility. Napoleon, however, saw fortified towns as playing an offensive role in "delay[ing], check[ing], weaken[ing], or harass[ing] an enemy conqueror," not merely repelling him. Such essentially offensive actions can be employed to set up an enemy force for counterattack.

Napoleon did all that he could to reduce war to what he called a science, but he drew the line at insisting on the absolute categorization of tactics into defensive or offensive. The most effective tactical leaders learn the accepted definitions and paradigms that apply to the tools and techniques they have at their disposal. Having learned them, however, they freely modify or even discard them altogether when circumstances or opportunities call for it.

Understand the "best practices" of your industry, but do not be imprisoned by them. Always be on the lookout for *another way*.

Lesson 13
Safety Real and Unreal

> "It is . . . in [a general's] boldness and stubbornness that the safety
> and conservation of men is found."
>
> ~ "Observations on the Wars of Marshal Turenne,"
> dictated by Napoleon at St. Helena, 1823

The first consideration of a general, according to Napoleon, is the "glory and honor of arms." The "safety and conservation" of his men is "only secondary." Harsh as this may seem, Napoleon continues by adding that it is in the general's "boldness and stubbornness that the safety and conservation of men is found."

Timidity in combat, an unwillingness to take bold, aggressive risks, a tendency to seek cover or initiate retreat rather than advance into danger, a fear of losing that is greater than a passion to win—all of these may be seen as flowing from a commander's desire to protect his men. In truth, however, such attitudes and values put an army at greater risk by demoralizing it, lulling it into a false sense of security, and rendering it unfit for combat, as well as prolonging a battle or a war and thereby increasing the time during which the army is in harm's way. Napoleon believed that true security comes from bold, decisive action, from attack rather than defense. An advancing army is a moving target and therefore harder to hit than a hunkered-down army. And bringing the battle to an enemy instead of waiting for the battle to come to you presents rather than accepts fear. Tactically, the most dangerous thing an army can do is to turn its back on an enemy. To retreat is to invite being shot in the back.

Avoiding danger by avoiding decisive action is often the most dangerous course into which a manager can lead her enterprise. The illusion of safety is far more dangerous than the known presence of real hazard.

Lesson 14

The Role of Experience

"Had I such a man as Turenne to assist me in my campaigns,
I would have been master of the world."

~ "Observations on the Wars of Marshal Turenne,"
dictated by Napoleon at St. Helena, 1823

Henri de la Tour d'Auvergne, Vicomte de Turenne (1611–75), was one of the great seventeenth-century marshals of France and a general whose campaigns Napoleon urged his own officers to "read and re-read." Napoleon compared Turenne to Louis, Prince of Condé, another great commander of the seventeenth century, but he concluded that whereas "le Grande Condé" was a "natural-born general, Turenne [was] a general by experience." Napoleon admired Turenne all the more for this, especially because he had "passed through all the grades, having been a soldier for one year, a captain for four, etc." It was his professional journey that had given him a thorough understanding of the military art.

Napoleon, the self-made emperor, valued experience—or, rather, what a person made of experience—far above genetic inheritance. He had high regard for Condé, the "natural-born" general, but thought much more highly of Turenne, the self-made general.

You are either a "born leader," or you are not. There is no choice in the matter. But to be a "leader by experience" is strictly a matter of choice, a decision you make to acquire experience, to learn from it, to master it, and to turn it to account in building a career. The examples of Turenne and Napoleon demonstrate that becoming a leader "by experience" is superior to the good fortune of having been born to it. In all endeavors, luck can take you only so far. Most of the journey is yours to make.

■

Lesson 15
Leadership: The Foremost Quality

> "The foremost quality of a commander is to keep a cool head, to receive accurate impressions of what is happening and never fret or be amazed or intoxicated by good news or bad."
>
> ~ "Summary of the Wars of Frederick II (the Great)," quoted in Jay Luvaas, *Napoleon on the Art of War*, 1999

For Napoleon, the prime requisite for command was the ability to see a situation clearly, uncolored by the emotions natural to war. He believed that both fear and elation colored and distorted the perception of reality. He knew from experience that a commander was assailed by many "successive or simultaneous sensations" during the course of a day, and he believed that a good commander possessed the ability to allow each to "occupy only as much attention" as each deserved. This faculty was important to preserve "common sense and good judgment," which, he believed, were the "products of a comparison of several sensations considered." No matter how intelligent or courageous a man was, if he did not possess a cool head, he was unfit to "command armies or to direct the great operations of war."

Objectivity, defined as a coolness of head that ensures undistorted situational awareness, is foremost among the qualities of a leader. Courage helps, but this "coolness" is not synonymous with courage. It is, rather, the faculty of maintaining clarity of vision even under great pressure, whether of fear or elation.

■

Lesson 16
The High Cost of Failing to Follow Through

> "At the commencement of a campaign, to advance or not to advance is a matter for grave consideration; but when once the offensive has been assumed, it must be sustained to the last extremity. However skillful the maneuvers in a retreat, it will always weaken the morale of an army, because in losing the chances of success these last are transferred to the enemy. Besides, retreats always cost more men and matériel than the most bloody engagements; with this difference, that in a battle the enemy's loss is nearly equal to your own—whereas in a retreat the loss is on your side only."
>
> ~Military Maxim VI, *The Military Maxims of Napoleon,* translated from the French by Lt. General Sir George C. D'Aguilar, 1831

Napoleon was not impulsive, and he did not equate boldness or audacity with acting on impulse. Deciding whether or not to advance was "a matter for grave consideration," not impulsive action. But once the advance had commenced, it became absolutely imperative to follow through, sustaining the offensive "to the last extremity." The reason for this was the high cost of retreat. An army is most vulnerable with its back to the enemy, typically suffering losses greater than those resulting from battle. Worse, the losses incurred in retreat buy nothing.

It takes a bold leader to initiate a high-stakes action. It takes a superb leader to sustain the boldness of the initial phase through to the end. Bold action carries risk, but the risk of failing to sustain boldness is far greater. Loss of momentum usually carries a high cost.

Lesson 17
Safety in Courage

> "In a retreat, besides the honor of the army, the loss of life is often greater than in two battles. For this reason, we should never despair while brave men are to be found with their colors. It is by this means we obtain victory, and deserve to obtain it."
>
> ~Military Maxim XV

The stock in trade of a general is hazard and risk. Misdirect your focus to safety, and the result will be a level of timidity that is ultimately more dangerous than defying death by boldly offering battle.

For soldiers and their commanders, the greatest security is in courage and action born of courage. Retreat, the product of fear, is the costliest maneuver an army can make, exposing its vulnerable flanks and rear to the enemy. Napoleon championed "glory and honor" not for their own sake, but for the victories they produced and what was ultimately the greater security they provided.

Fear may drive us to seek safety, but it does not provide safety. A decision based on fear is the most dangerous a leader can make because it sacrifices confidence, hope, opportunity, and rational decision-making. Fear simultaneously demands reaction while limiting or even denying positive action. Fear is surrender, which forecloses on victory.

Lesson 18

If You Want to Be Victorious, Act Like a Winner

> "A general of ordinary talent occupying a bad position, and sur-
> prised by a superior force, seeks his safety in retreat; but a great
> captain supplies all deficiencies by his courage, and marches
> boldly to meet the attack. By this means he disconcerts his adver-
> sary; and if the latter shows any irresolution in his movements, a
> skillful leader, profiting by his indecision, may even hope for vic-
> tory, or at least employ the day in maneuvering—at night he
> entrenches himself, or falls back to a better position. By this deter-
> mined conduct he maintains the honor of his arms, the first essen-
> tial to all military superiority."
>
> ~ Military Maxim XVIII

At the core of Napoleon's military genius was his willingness and
ability to act in ways that shaped reality to conform to his vision of
reality, even under the most adverse circumstances. No one understood the power of audacity better than Napoleon. He understood
that an ordinary general, "occupying a bad position, and surprised
by a superior force, seeks his safety in retreat," whereas he, Napoleon, would instead march "boldly to meet the attack."

Such an unexpected action was neither a suicide mission
nor a simple gamble. On the contrary, it represented the best
hope and most rational action for a commander at a disadvantage, because:

1. Audacious action disconcerted—or even stunned—
   the enemy.

2. It lured the enemy into "irresolution in his movements,"
   errors that could be exploited to great advantage.

3. It kept the fight going and options open. As long as an
   army has men and can maneuver, it has rational hope.
   Retreat, however, is inherently hopeless.

4. It maintained "honor of arms," possession of which made an army an army. And, an army is always capable of victory.

> **Both victory and defeat**—success and failure—begin as self-proclaimed judgments. If you start out like the winner and continue to resist the urge to act like the loser, there is a good chance that you will be rewarded with success. There are no guarantees, except the certainty that costly failure begins with your decision to retreat.

■

Lesson 19
Be Aggressive in Preserving Your Options

"When you are occupying a position which the enemy threatens to surround, collect all your force immediately, and menace him with an offensive movement. By this maneuver you will prevent him from detaching and annoying your flanks, in case you should judge it necessary to retire."

~ Military Maxim XXIII

Napoleon used bold offensive tactics not only to defeat an enemy army and capture enemy territory, but also to preserve his options. As he saw it, surrendering freedom of movement was even worse than losing soldiers or giving ground. As long as a general could maneuver his army, he possessed the means to victory.

> **No calculated risk** is too great except one that sacrifices your ability to act on your own best judgment.

■

Lesson 20

To Protect Your Assets, Use Your Assets

"Artillery should always be placed in the most advantageous positions, and as far in front of the line of cavalry and infantry as possible, without compromising the safety of the guns.

"Field batteries should command the whole country round from the level of the platform. They should on no account be masked on the right and left, but have free range in every direction."

~ Military Maxim LIV

In the Napoleonic era, artillery was the great prize in any battle. One side always tried to destroy or, far better, to capture the other side's guns. As with any treasure, the commonsense impulse was to hide and guard precious artillery, but Napoleon considered this attitude the height of folly.

While valueless if destroyed or captured, artillery was equally without value unless it was used and used well. This meant bringing it as far in front as you dared and positioning it out in the open, where it commanded "free range in every direction." To be sure, this exposed your guns to the possibility of capture; however, if you used them well and vigorously, the guns themselves prevented their loss.

The hard fact of war is that, to deliver a defeat, you must expose yourself to the very possibility of defeat.

Invest in resources that produce value even at the cost of risking those very resources. Whatever fails to produce value is a liability, whether you call it an asset, a valuable, a treasure, or a cannon.

■

Lesson 21
Try Obstinacy

> "Great extremities require extraordinary resolution. The more
> obstinate the resistance of an army, the greater the chances of
> assistance or of success."
>
> ~ Military Maxim LXVII

Although justly celebrated as a master of tactics and strategy,
Napoleon actually believed that his most powerful leadership
resource was his own resolution and his ability to impart commensurate stubbornness to his army. In Napoleon's view, it was
the sheer will to persist and resist that most dramatically multiplied an army's chances for victory. Such obstinacy would result
either in triumph or delay defeat long enough to receive assis-
tance and reinforcement.

Defeat requires surrender, a decision that, in most cases,
comes long before it has to. Your adversary has the same
choice to make as you do, namely whether to persist in the
fight or to give up. Do whatever you can to outlast an opponent, and you increase the chance that he will give up before
you do. Give up, and you end all chance of victory. Obstinacy is
a valid—and powerful—leadership option.

■

Lesson 22
Do or Die

> "How many seeming impossibilities have been accomplished by men whose only resolve was death!"
>
> ~ Military Maxim LXVII

Backed against a wall, an army responds either with uncoordinated panic or an apparently superhuman resolve that accomplishes "seeming impossibilities." Napoleon knew that the choice to do or die was a risky one, but he regarded it as by far the most potent version of his favorite command quality, *audacity*. It was the power Caesar found when he crossed the Rubicon, making an irreversible decision for a civil war that he either had to win or, by losing, suffer certain death.

Few incentives are more powerful than a stark choice. *Either we make the project succeed, or we're all out of a job.* But like any powerful force, do-or-die must be given shape and direction by a strong leader, lest the enterprise be overwhelmed either by the spirit of every man for himself or the chaos induced by sheer panic. Effective leadership under do-or-die circumstances requires flawless judgment, limitless resolve, and powerful charisma.

■

Lesson 23
Bear the Burden

> "Few people realize the strength of mind required to conduct, with a
> full realization of its consequences, one of these great battles on which
> depends the fate of an army, a nation, the possession of a throne."
>
> ~Napoleon in exile at St. Helena,
> quoted in Felix Markham, *Napoleon*, 1963

Napoleon has often been stereotyped as an aggressive tyrant who
undertook military conquest with an almost casually impulsive
rapacity, but the evidence reveals a very different character. Napoleon was in fact acutely aware of the colossal stakes of the campaigns
he undertook and found them a heavy burden to bear. Hardly the
egomaniac he is so often portrayed to be, Napoleon always understood just what hung in the balance with every campaign.

When he reflected, during his final exile, that most people
had no conception of the "strength of mind" required to conduct a
great battle, he did not expect sympathy or pity for himself. Instead,
he was at pains to explain that his willingness to "give battle" had
always been founded on his willingness to accept the awful
burdens of his actions. Such willingness, he insisted, was rare,
which meant that "generals who are willing to give battle" were
few and far between.

Whatever else leadership is, it is above all else the willingness
to accept responsibilities extending far beyond oneself. The
pinnacle of any career, leadership is at the same time a heavy
burden. The weight is not a part of the job, it is the very essence
of the job.

■

Lesson 24
Two O'Clock in the Morning Courage

> "I have rarely met with that 'two o'clock in the morning courage';
> in other words, spontaneous courage which is necessary on some
> unexpected occasion and which permits full freedom of judgment
> and decision despite the most unforeseen events."
> ~Napoleon, quoted in Emmanuel-Augustin-Dieudonné-Joseph,
> comte de Las Cases, *Mémorial de Ste. Hélène*, 1823

One of Napoleon's most widely quoted phrases, "two o'clock in the morning courage," referred to courage that came naturally and was unrehearsed. It was a form of courage present even at the loneliest time of night, the time in which one's thoughts, focused inward, are often in danger of turning toward anxiety or even outright panic.

Napoleon saw physical courage as part and parcel of the soldier's chosen way of life, and he simply expected it from himself and others of his profession. Intellectual and moral courage, however, were different, and much harder to come by. These qualities intrigued him far more than common physical courage, and they seemed to him a rare and precious commodity. They enabled a leader to make quick, accurate decisions at any time and under any circumstances, decisions involving the fate of many others—perhaps an army or an entire nation—in addition to himself.

Possession of "two o'clock in the morning courage" may be the ultimate test of one's readiness to lead. It is not fearlessness, but, far more important, the ability to make decisions undistorted by whatever fear, fatigue, and depression one feels.

■

2

Vision
and
Strategy

Lesson 25
Ride the Tide

> "The [French] revolution is the mistress of the hour. One cannot struggle against it, one must accommodate oneself to it."
> ~Letter to Alexandre des Mazis, August 1792

The French Revolution, which sent so many prominent young men to the guillotine, was the making of Napoleon Bonaparte. There was nevertheless much about it that he detested, including the mob mentality and mob actions, the execution of Louis XVI, and the bloody madness of the Terror. But, for him, there was no acceptable alternative to the Revolution—certainly not a return to monarchy or to feudal rule by individual lords. The Revolution was a fact and, as he explained to his young aristocratic friend Alexandre des Mazis, it was not to be resisted.

But neither was it to be surrendered to.

Instead, Napoleon observed, "one must accommodate oneself to it." The reward for doing this successfully was not merely survival but unprecedented and virtually limitless advancement.

Discriminate among cultural and commercial ripples, waves, and tides. The first you can safely ignore, while the second two require your attention. You may need to stand against a wave or allow it to carry you where it will, but a tide cannot be resisted. You have the choice of being swallowed up and drowned or of riding it, adapting to it, and making profitable use of it as you would any other vehicle.

■

Lesson 26
Attack the Keystone

> "Concentrate your fire against a single point, and once the wall
> is breached all of the rest becomes worthless and the fortress is
> captured."
>
> ~ "Notes on the Political and Military Position of Our Armies
> in Piedmont and Spain, June 1794," quoted in Jay Luvaas,
> *Napoleon on the Art of War*, 1999

From his earliest days as a commander, Napoleon sought to ratio-
nalize the violent force of war to gain the greatest result with the
least expenditure of men, equipment, and other resources. For him,
this was both the purpose and essence of strategy.

Called on to advise the revolutionary government of France
on how and whom to fight for the very survival of the nation, Napoleon declared it "essential not to scatter our attacks but to concentrate them."

But concentrate them on what?

The overall purpose of the wars of the Revolution was to
protect France from invasion; therefore, he deduced, the "general
principle of our war is to defend the frontiers." He next asked
which of the powers arrayed in coalition against France presented
the greatest threat to French frontiers. The answer was Austria,
and so the overall strategy of the war must be "to see that the
different [French] armies strike their blows, directly or indirectly,
against this power." An offensive war on France's frontier with
Spain, Napoleon explained, would be "separate and distinct" from
war against Austria and its closest ally, Germany. Neither Austria
nor Germany would "feel any effects from it"; however, a French
offensive in Piedmont would force Austria to defend its Italian
states "and consequently this plan would be in the general character of our war."

Napoleon explained that deciding what war to fight, what enemy to choose, was like attacking a fortress. The attacking army did not direct its fire all along the fortress wall because the commander knew that this would simply dilute the effect of the fire. Instead, it concentrated its fire on a single point. The object was not to knock down the whole wall, but merely to breach it. Breach a wall, and the entire fortress will surrender. "It is Germany [by which Napoleon meant Austria and the German states allied with Austria against France] that must be crushed; once this is accomplished Spain and Italy will fall by themselves. Therefore it is essential not to scatter our attacks but to concentrate them [against Austria]."

Strategy begins and ends with the effective allocation of resources. In attacking any problem, no matter how complex, use strategic planning to identify the keystone. This is not necessarily the weakest point. On the contrary, it may be the strongest point—the thorniest issue in the problem you are attacking. Nevertheless, concentrate effectively against it, and the entire arch will fall. Throwing resources randomly against a problem is rarely a sustainable business policy. Practice a strategic economy that targets the keystones or the points at which the greatest leverage can be achieved.

■

Lesson 27
Give Direction to Courage

> "A central authority [should devote] its full powers . . . by profound insight [to give] direction to courage and [thereby make] our success substantial, decisive, and less bloody."
>
> ~ "Notes on the Political and Military Position of Our Armies in Piedmont and Spain, June 1794," quoted in Jay Luvaas, *Napoleon on the Art of War*, 1999

While still a relatively junior officer, Napoleon was assigned to report on the military needs of the French revolutionary government's forces in the Italian Piedmont and Spain.

He began by analyzing the current situation of the armies, noting that they were generally insufficient to fight an offensive war. Instead of simply recommending that the armies be reinforced and built up, however, he urged the government to create an overall strategy, because each army needed to be manned and equipped to wage "a kind of war relative to the overall plan for the war."

An overall strategy, Napoleon reasoned, including clear war aims, can come only from the highest authority in the government. From this authorized strategy flow all orders for the composition, deployment, and mission of each army. If "courage" is the raw energy of a military force, it is the responsibility of the central authority to create a "stable system" whereby an effective strategy is created for the purpose of giving "direction to courage."

The enterprise looks to its leader for a strategy founded on rational principles for comprehensible goals. Your role is to give "direction to the courage" of your organization. Energy is useless unless it is directed to do useful work, and such direction, in the form of a rational strategy, must be in place before the organization is finally staffed and equipped. Strategy directs not only the work of the enterprise, but the very structure of the company.

Lesson 28
The First Necessity

> "Unity of command is of the first necessity in war."
>
> ~ "Notes on the Art of War," quoted in Jay Luvaas,
> *Napoleon on the Art of War*, 1999

Napoleon had wide-ranging military ambitions, but he sought to fight one battle at a time, concentrating as many troops as possible on the battlefield so that he could "take advantage of every opportunity." Today, the metaphor he famously employed strikes us as a sexist cliché, but it does capture his seize-the-moment approach to progress: "Fortune is a woman: if you miss her today, do not expect to find her tomorrow."

Of equal importance to concentrating troops to exploit opportunity was unity of command. Writing to the Directory on May 14, 1796, during the Italian campaign, Napoleon protested the notion of dividing the Army of Italy in two and placing "two different generals in command." He implored the Directory to have but "one general who possesses your complete confidence," and he pledged to "redouble [his] zeal to earn [your] esteem in the position that you confide to me." He admitted that General François-Etienne Kellermann, with whom the Directory wanted him to share command, had more experience than he and might even lead the army better. But, Napoleon warned, "the two of us together would be a disaster. It would be better to have one poor general than two good ones." In the interests of achieving "speed in movements and as much quickness in conception as in execution," Napoleon insisted on achieving "unity of thought"—and perfect unity of thought could only be had with a single general in command.

Napoleon always sought to consolidate and concentrate resources, both physical (the army) and mental (the command). By refusing to share command, he tried always to keep his army united geographically as well as operationally. The great enemy of strategically effective planning and tactically effective execution is vagueness or diversity of command. The activities of the enterprise should flow from a single authoritative decision maker.

■

Lesson 29
No Victory without Discipline

"Without discipline there is no victory."

~Order of the Day, June 11, 1796

Like an army, an armed mob kills people and breaks things. The critical difference between the two is discipline, which included, according to Napoleon, respect for property. Pillage and theft, he warned his soldiers, "belong only to the cowardly."

Although Napoleon was often slandered as a latter-day Attila, his greatest and most enduring victories depended not on conquest alone but also on improving the lives of the people living in the territories he acquired. He tempered conquest with ethics.

His objective in battle was victory, but this did not require his opponent to be utterly defeated. For him, war was not necessarily a zero-sum game. Napoleon often looked for compromise and mutual benefit. He believed, when possible, in exchanging value for value rather than merely seizing what he wanted. This approach required sufficient discipline to restrain both his own ambitions as well as his soldiers' natural inclination to destroy and pillage. While he wanted to impose his vision of order on the world, he wanted the world to accept it willingly, and not merely out of fear. Voluntary compliance is always more economical than coerced and enforced obedience. The one asks for acceptance, the other requires the continual application of force—and that is a costly proposition that makes conquest unsustainable.

To be sustainable, a business must consistently return value for value received. A sustainable business does not force its vision on others but instead embraces a highly disciplined system of exchange that produces willing cooperation, collaboration, and compliance.

■

Lesson 30
The Most Valuable Commodity

"The loss of time is irreparable in war."
~Letter to General Barthélemy-Catherine Joubert, February 17, 1797

Of all things needful in war—or any other enterprise—only time is absolutely finite. Spent, time is lost. And lost, time cannot be regained.

In war, the consequence of lost time is often defeat. Napoleon believed that "operations misfire only through delays." Thus, as he saw it, time was the sovereign fuel of strategy, tactics, and execution alike. Indeed, time was so powerful an element that the art of war, for Napoleon, consisted "simply in gaining time when one has inferior forces."

All planning must begin and end with time—the one dimension of an enterprise that cannot be changed. It can and must, however, be managed. Whereas delay can be costly or even fatal, intelligent management of time can be used to leverage all other resources and thereby augment the bottom line. For example, any number of just-in-time (JIT) strategies can be employed to ensure that supplies or merchandise are available only when needed, to keep warehousing and handling costs to a minimum. Seasonal adjustments to the workforce are another example of leveraging time to reduce costs. Because time is relentless, its management is among the most crucial tasks any business leader takes on.

Lesson 31
Never Settle

> "Because our way of making war is so different."
>
> ~Letter to the Directory, January 20, 1797

Napoleon's brilliant victories in the first Italian campaign put him in position to complete his transformation of the Army of Italy from a neglected and undermanned backwater military mob into the foremost military force of revolutionary France. He had long needed reinforcements, and he now had the record of achievement the Directory demanded before it would furnish them. A conventional commander would have been happy to get whatever men he could to build up what was still a very small army. Napoleon, however, boldly insisted that the Directory send him only the very best officers—the cream of the officer corps—together with the best young troops available. His justification for this demand was that "our way of making war is so different" from that of other armies and generals. His was a "war of movements and maneuvers," a kind of war that had brought "great successes," but a kind of war that required great generals, great officers, and great soldiers. Such was the case he successfully presented to an always-reluctant Directory.

Conventional managers always think more about costs and constraints than they do about opportunity and possibility. As a result, they often settle for whatever they can get, including the hiring and development of merely adequate instead of truly outstanding employees.

Such managers aim no higher than "filling a slot" and "keeping things moving" and may argue that one must not let the best become the enemy of the good.

It is a depressing and dangerous argument. Rather than resort to it, shift your emphasis to the positive—like Napoleon, from defense to offense, from cost to opportunity, from constraint to possibility. Make this mental shift, and you will be less likely to settle. Consistently demand the best—invest in it—and you will encounter fewer and fewer situations that tempt you to settle for less.

■

Lesson 32
Define True Power

"True conquests, the only ones which leave no regret, are those made over ignorance."

~Napoleon's speech accepting membership in the National
Institute of Sciences and Arts, December 26, 1797

The Napoleonic Wars wrote history in blood. Territories, states, and entire peoples moved from one leader to another, one government to another. Until the twentieth century, with its Bolshevik revolution, two world wars, and Cold War, no one leader or group of leaders had so great an impact on global geopolitics and humanity as Napoleon.

Yet it was not these bloody conquests—a matter of guns and military strategy—that Napoleon counted as his "true" achievements. Napoleon was an intensely curious man with a great interest in philosophy and science. He included prominent scientists among his official advisers and treasured his membership in the National Institute of Sciences and Arts. He believed the most meaningful battlefield was the human mind, and he wanted France not merely to hold land and people under its dominion, but to lead the advancement of the mind itself. "The most honorable and useful occupation for nations," he told the members of the Institute, "is to contribute to the extension of human knowledge. The true power of the French Republic should consist henceforth in allowing no single new idea to escape its embrace."

The power of a business is typically measured in money—money made, money to be made, money controlled, money at risk, money owed, money lost. The sources of a firm's wealth may be many: patents held, mines owned, loans made, services sold, real estate possessed—the list is long. At root, however, there is but a single source of business power. It is the claim a company has on some aspect of the human mind that prompts people to invest in whatever the enterprise offers. Emulate Napoleon the conqueror. Aim to acquire as much of this mental real estate as you can.

■

Lesson 33
The Right Way to Deal with Defeat

> "If defeated he [Marshal André Masséna] would start again as if he had been the victor."
>
> ~ "Italian Campaigns," quoted in Jay Luvaas,
> *Napoleon on the Art of War*, 1999

Nothing, it would seem, could be more certain than defeat. Yet it is precisely this apparently self-evident proposition that the great generals have most consistently rejected. Napoleon cited his own Marshal Masséna as a case in point, but Americans may be more familiar with Ulysses S. Grant or George S. Patton Jr. Grant suffered one costly tactical defeat after another at the hands of Robert E. Lee in the Civil War, but he responded to each not by retreating, as a defeated general is supposed to, but as if he had been victorious. With each reverse, he advanced farther south, forcing Lee to spend more of his dwindling army against him.

During World War II, General Patton put this approach in a single simple directive: "You aren't beaten until you quit. Hence, don't."

Failure is a fact compounded of reality and perception. Even when the externals point to your defeat, you can choose to maintain control over perception. How you respond to a reversal of fortune determines whether it will be a wall, a cliff, or a door.

■

Lesson 34
The Morality of Obedience

"If the general understands the benefit and consequently the morality of [a] strange . . . order, he must execute it. If he does not understand it, however, he should not obey."

~ "Observations on the Campaigns of 1796 and 1797," quoted in Jay Luvaas, *Napoleon on the Art of War*, 1999

Napoleon never took the nature of command for granted, so he thought long and hard about the moral limits of obedience. If the supreme commander clearly, unmistakably, and absolutely issued a "strange" order—say, to make an attack that even he admitted was doomed—insisting that the order was his will and therefore had to be obeyed, the subordinate was required to obey only if he understood the *benefit* (and therefore the *morality*) of the order. In the absence of this understanding, however, Napoleon was firm in his conviction that he should refuse to execute the order.

Orders are executed for the benefit of the enterprise, not in unthinking submission to the boss's will.

■

Lesson 35
Value Is a Matter of Common Sense

> "To make supernatural efforts to cross unapproachable moun-
> tains and then find oneself still in the middle of precipices, defiles,
> and boulders . . . is to act contrary to common sense and therefore
> is contrary to the spirit of the art of war."
>
> ~ "Memoirs of the Campaigns of Egypt and Syria,
> dictated by Napoleon at St. Helena," quoted in
> Jay Luvaas, *Napoleon on the Art of War*, 1999

An invasion, Napoleon believed, should be accomplished by the easiest, most direct means possible, and it should target the enemy's "cities, beautiful provinces, and capitals"—the true prizes of invasion. While threatening such treasures would surely meet with resistance, invading via the most difficult routes in an effort to avoid resistance violates common sense. To invade a country is to put your military and political assets at great risk in order to gain something of greater value. Its purpose is not to enter a country by the easiest possible route for the purpose of possessing its least valuable assets.

Deciding whether attaining a certain objective is worth what you have to risk or spend to get it must begin and end with common sense. If the objective requires an investment that clearly exceeds the value of what will be gained, either you must find a cheaper means of attaining the objective or you must find another objective. Reject any preconceived notions, traditions, or wishful thinking that drive you to make value decisions in violation of common sense.

■

Lesson 36

Finding a Reason for War

> "It could be advantageous for the [French] republic to make the conquest of Egypt pave the way for a glorious peace with England."
>
> ~Letter to the Executive Directory [revolutionary French governing authority], October 7, 1798

No episode of Napoleon's military career is more controversial than his Egyptian campaign. Many biographers and historians have asserted that waging war in Egypt was a monumental instance of overreaching, putting a great deal at risk for an obscure reward.

Perhaps.

The campaign was certainly costly, and Napoleon ultimately abandoned it. Nevertheless, the Egyptian expedition goes to the core of his visionary concept of strategy.

Some wars, especially those of the French revolutionary period, were thrust upon Napoleon. Others he instigated with the clear objective of immediate conquest. But in the case of Egypt, Napoleon actively sought a reason for war, then vigorously sold that reason to the Directory. He first claimed that the Ottoman government, which controlled Egypt, had repeatedly insulted French sovereignty, even imprisoning French consuls in Egypt. That was one reason for war, but Napoleon doubted that the Directory would find it sufficient. He therefore continued by making a case for conquest based on Egypt's possession of the "most beautiful [soil] on earth" (which made it desirable) and on the divided loyalties of its peoples (which made it conquerable).

But he reserved for last his most compelling argument for war, probably the only one that really interested him. The location of Egypt was, he said, "decisive for India," adding the "European nation that controls Egypt will, in the long run, control India." This was itself valuable, but Napoleon drove home its importance by suggesting that putting France in position to control India by conquering Egypt would necessarily "pave the way for a glorious peace with England." He understood that India was the jewel in the crown of Britain's empire. Threaten it, and England would have no choice but to come to favorable terms with France.

> **Napoleonic strategy is** visionary and global. From it, we learn to see strategy in grandly systemic and elaborately networked terms and come to understand that pressure applied in one place can have a profound effect in another. To execute global strategy, it is necessary to understand the system of linkages involved in any proposed action and, what is more, to possess the ability to persuade others of these linkages and the local benefits of apparently remote actions. Global strategies are not only the most difficult to execute, but almost always the hardest to understand and, therefore, to promote persuasively.

■

Lesson 37
Free, Don't Tie, Your Hands

"A Constitution should be short—and obscure."
~Napoleon, quoted in Felix Markham, *Napoleon*, 1963

Taking a hand in the creation of the French government at the start of 1800, Napoleon put into practice his prescription for the writing of a constitution: Make it short and make it obscure. In part, this was a move to get a new Republican constitution before the people as quickly as possible and to avoid touching off endless dispute about details. More important, however, was Napoleon's desire to escape the constraints of the written word on his freedom to govern as he wanted. A short and obscure constitution would impose the color of law on his government without limiting his ability to interpret the document in ways that enabled rather than hobbled his will. Government guided by a sketch rather than a fully finished painting left him ample room for improvisation and adaptation in response to and in anticipation of real-world challenges, crises, and opportunities.

The notion that rules are made to be broken creates cynical governance lacking in credibility. Far better to avoid creating rules that you later may need to break. Consider a model of governance that articulates nothing more detailed than certain aims, objectives, and principles, the execution of which is left open, more a matter of improvisation than of prescription. Governing documents should enable far more than they constrain.

■

Lesson 38
Win in the Other Guy's Mind

"In the Moravian campaign [of 1806] I understood that the Russians, having no general of the first rank, would believe that the French army would retreat upon Vienna. They had to make it a high priority to intercept this road, when in fact the retreat of the [French] army throughout the Moravian campaign had never been intended to be toward Vienna. This single circumstance distorted all of the enemy's calculations and inevitably contributed to those movements that led to his defeat."

~ "Official After-action Report of the Battle of Austerlitz,"
March 28, 1806

Like Robert E. Lee and George S. Patton Jr., Napoleon possessed an uncanny ability to see a battle from the perspective of his adversary and thereby play out in his mind the enemy's likely moves. He shaped this exercise of sympathetic imagination largely on the basis of his estimation of his opponent's ability or lack thereof. This enabled him to make an informed guess about the key moves the enemy would make. With this knowledge, Napoleon was able to outmaneuver the enemy and concentrate on its weakest points.

> **When competing against** an internal or external rival, learn all that you can about her. Seek patterns in her past moves. Endeavor to evaluate her level of skill, boldness, and innovation. Examine her track record. Compile an informal dossier—at least in your mind—and use it to put yourself in her place. Imagine her moves. Plan yours accordingly. Prepare and position yourself to exploit errors, weaknesses, and vulnerabilities.

■

Lesson 39
Leave Nothing to Chance

> "My habit is to leave nothing to chance."
> ~ Letter to General Joachim Murat, March 14, 1808

Generals Ulysses S. Grant and William Tecumseh Sherman believed that their campaign-planning responsibilities began and ended with their own armies. It was futile, they asserted, to attempt to fight the enemy's battle as well as your own. Napoleon would have rejected this approach. He believed that war and battle planning were essentially matters of "calculation," of calculating your objectives and the movements necessary to achieve them *balanced against* your calculation of the enemy's likely objectives, movements, and counter-movements. The result of this double set of calculations was "many precautions" that flowed from Napoleon's "habit" of leaving "nothing to chance."

Napoleon's standard of planning was to create a "plan of campaign" that "anticipate[s] everything that the enemy can do"—not merely is *likely* to do—and to "contain with it the means of out-maneuvering him." What he called "calculation" was the product of a detailed sympathetic imagination, a kind of earnest war-gaming in which he played both sides. The alternative to this level of planning was either failure or the hope of success "through some freak of fortune." Neither was acceptable to Napoleon.

Napoleon believed in what he called freaks of fortune, but he refused to trust in them. His goal in planning a campaign was always to minimize the role of chance—ideally to "leave nothing to chance." The only way to progress toward this ideal goal is to replace the unknown with the known or, at the very least, with the probable and the plausible. This is done through planning that takes into account not only your own objectives and resources, but those of clients and adversaries as well. Intelligence based on reliable data is the best way to fill in the blanks concerning others, but where this is missing, an exercise of informed sympathetic imagination is called for. Put yourself in the place of your clients as well as your competitors.

■

Lesson 40
Think Small

> "I strongly recommend that you have the troops maneuver as much in small groups as in the school of the battalion, so that they are accustomed to deploy rapidly while those who come in ranks perform fire by files."
>
> ~Letter to Marshal Jean-Baptiste Bessières, May 25, 1808

In the days of single-shot, muzzle-loading muskets, weapons were discharged in a simultaneous volley by one line of troops while the line or lines standing behind them reloaded and prepared to fire a second volley. Understandably, therefore, commanders drilled their troops to move in unison, form a line of fire, fire, then withdraw in orderly fashion behind what had been the second line to reload while that second line—now in front—fired their volley.

It was a complex set of maneuvers, but it could all be learned by rote. The problem was that it produced soldiers virtually incapable of coherent and rapid individual and small-unit actions. Napoleon sought to remedy this by putting as much emphasis on small-unit drill as on conventional battalion-size drill. His objective was to achieve not just orderly deployment but rapid deployment and a high degree of self-reliance.

Most generals did not think or plan below the regimental level. Battalion and company maneuvers were relegated to lower-level officers. Napoleon, in contrast, devoted attention not just to armies and corps, but also to small units, down to the company or even the individual soldier. His vision might have been telescopic, capable of imagining global conquest, but it was also microscopic, intimately involved in the details of the execution of even the most ambitious of plans.

To think big, think small. Engage all elements of your enterprise at the elemental level. Understand how each group works and who is on each team. Get to know each of the people in whose hands you place the realization of your vision. Although the movements you plan may be grand, their success depends on the agility and efficiency of each group, team, and individual assigned to carry the project forward. Equip these "small" units to carry the load you assign to them. Never dismiss "mere details."

Lesson 41
The Self-Sustaining Enterprise

"War must nourish war."

~Letter to Marshal Louis-Alexandre Berthier, May 29, 1810

Napoleon's most often-quoted maxim is perhaps "An army travels on its stomach." Celebrated as a visionary strategist and tactical genius, Napoleon's greatest concern was first and last logistical: how to sustain his armies in the field. While he formulated systems of fortified towns and fortresses to serve as depots along the route of an advance, he ultimately relied on an army's ability to live off the land.

Napoleon employed a combination of means to make "war . . . nourish war." Whenever and wherever possible, he emulated Alexander the Great and Julius Caesar, making it profitable for the people he conquered to supply him with food, clothing, shelter, and even weapons and ammunition. When a population proved recalcitrant, however, Napoleon acted with the full brutality of a conqueror and simply took what he needed.

For Napoleon the ultimate objective of war was to enrich France, both geopolitically and economically. When he had the Directory to answer to, Napoleon saw to it that his armies sent a steady stream of loot back to Paris. He knew that war was costly, and that the government would continue to support it only as long as it produced revenue. As Napoleon's concepts of campaigning matured, however, he looked beyond looting and sought to devise policies that would make war self-sustaining. The conquerors—the looters—would always feed themselves.

The idea of investing money in an enterprise that will produce revenue at some later time is a business model so well established that it is rarely questioned. But more than two hundred years ago, this is precisely what Napoleon questioned.

Emulate Napoleon's ideal of nourishing war with war by

creating strategies that nourish enterprise with enterprise. Instead of dividing major projects into compartmentalized phases of "investment" and "return," devise ways in which some of the return may be integrated into the investment. This may be achieved by calling for marketable deliverables in the research and development phase of a project. Such deliverables might be smaller products created in the course of developing a bigger product, or they may be internal deliverables, such as tools and procedures that contribute to the work of the entire organization, including work groups and teams occupied with their own development projects. *R&D must nourish R&D.*

■

Lesson 42
Never Allow Assets to Become Liabilities

"Prepare a plan. . . . War consists of unforeseen events."
~ Letter to General Henri-Jacques-Guillaume Clarke,
November 12, 1811

Napoleon regarded heavy cavalry—large men armored with steel breastplates, riding large horses, and armed with heavy sabers and carbines—as the most effective units of his cavalry and among his greatest assets. Yet they were also vulnerable within their encampments if surprised by a lightning attack conducted by unarmored riders with light carbines and sabers or other less formidably armed troops.

"I cannot get used to seeing 3,000 elite men," Napoleon wrote to General Clarke, being wiped out by "light troops . . . a partisan, or . . . some inferior marksmen behind some stream or house. This is absurd." But the truth was that, when not mounted and actually fighting, the heavy cavalry was vulnerable. The great military asset became a burdensome military liability.

The conventional approach to protecting heavy cavalry in camp was to assign an infantry guard to it. To Napoleon, monopolizing troops for the sole purpose of protecting other troops was as "absurd" as the idea of heavy cavalry being defeated by light cavalry or by partisans (lightly armed guerrilla or popular militia troops). He instructed General Clarke, therefore, to prepare "a plan . . . so that these 3,000 men have no need of infantry to guard them." He recommended training the heavy cavalry to fight dismounted in camp–to act as its own defensive infantry. Not that he ever wanted his heavy cavalry employed primarily as a defensive force. That would be a waste of the army's fiercest, best-equipped, and most formidable horses and riders. But it would be no great undertaking, he reasoned, to train and equip heavy cavalry units to provide their own defense.

"War consists of unforeseen events, not in having assumptions that 15,000 heavy cavalry must always be kept in such a way as to be protected." To make such an assumption is to turn an asset into at least a partial liability–to transform a weapon of war into a mere valuable possession that requires protection, thereby draining the strength of the army instead of adding to it. For Napoleon, self-sufficiency was the best means of ensuring that an asset remains an asset.

Always bear in mind the great difference between *riches* and *wealth*. To be rich is to possess at a certain time and a certain place things of great value. To be wealthy is to possess the ongoing means of creating more wealth. Riches require protection—an expenditure of resources. Riches therefore consist of liabilities. Wealth consists of assets, the engines of wealth. Invest in assets—commodities that produce revenue—rather than liabilities, valuables that require protection and other costly servicing.

■

Lesson 43
Establish Your Position

> "War is a profession of positions."
>
> ~Letter to Marshal Auguste-Frédéric-Louis Marmont,
> February 18, 1812

"An army defeated and thrown back into the desert can no longer take a position," Napoleon wrote during his Egyptian campaign of 1798. For an army to take a position, there must be a position to take—a place offering food, water, shelter, and defensible cover from which to repel the enemy. The desert offered none of these.

Napoleon understood that an army maneuvered into warfare on the open desert gives up the possibility of establishing a position. As he saw it, an army must not simply fight, it must fight from a readily defended place. He always insisted on amassing all the advantages in battle: better generals, better soldiers, and a better position. Of the three, he often considered position the most important.

Positioning **has long** been key in the art of marketing. It is the means and process by which you create an identity for your product in the minds of existing and potential customers. Few companies are content simply to put their merchandise "out there" and see who comes to it waving dollar bills. The more effective and efficient way of selling is to carve out a position in the minds of consumers and then to create product design, advertising, and pricing that reinforces that position and defends it against encroachment by competitors.

You don't have to be vending merchandise to benefit from the concept of positioning. If you aspire to leadership, the first requirement is to deliver excellent performance at all times. The second requirement is to ensure that this record of performance favorably positions you in the minds of your bosses, colleagues, clients, and subordinates as a leader, the go-to problem solver, and the practical visionary.

Associate yourself with projects that offer opportunity, not defeat. Make connections with the most influential people in the organization. Don't avoid colleagues you perceive as competitors; connect with them, work with them. Don't worry that your subordinates are after your job; mentor them, work to promote them into positions of authority. They will help you put your stamp on the organization, and that, in turn, positions you for leadership.

If you fail to establish a position, others will do it for you. And you are unlikely to benefit from the result.

■

Lesson 44
Cover Your Rear

"It is contrary to every principle . . . to defend the head of the convoy in preference to the rest of it. . . . The tail is the point of greatest need of protection, since the enemy always attacks here."
~ Letter to Marshal Louis-Alexandre Berthier, May 27, 1813

Most commanders in the Napoleonic era led supply convoys with an armed escort. After reviewing his own long experience of campaigning, however, it was clear to Napoleon that convoys are not typically headed off by the enemy, but attacked from the rear, where they are most vulnerable—especially if the bulk of the escort is far to the front of the column. Although seeing the escort ahead of them made transport troops feel more comfortable, Napoleon ordered most of the escort to be concentrated in the rear, where it was most needed.

It is human nature to look ahead for danger. In any high-stakes enterprise, however, the greatest danger often lies behind, the point from which you least expect it. Do not base the allocation of resources on what makes you feel secure but on what will

actually enable you and your organization to address vulnerabilities and exploit opportunities, even if you have to venture
outside of your comfort zone.

■

Lesson 45
The Place for Artillery

"Never forget that in war all artillery must be with the army and
not in the park."
~ Letter to General Henri-Jacques-Guillaume Clarke,
January 18, 1814

"Had I possessed 30,000 artillery rounds at Leipzig on the evening
of 18 October, today I would be master of the world."

But Napoleon didn't, and so he was defeated by the coalition
of states arrayed against him. The following year, the Battle of
Waterloo would send him into exile.

Artillery in the "park"—its place of encampment—can achieve
nothing. Only when it is properly deployed with the army in
action does it serve a productive purpose. Potential energy, no
matter how great, does no work. All achievement is the result
of kinetic energy. Leadership is all about having what you need
in action where and when you need it.

■

Lesson 46
Strategy Begins with What You Have

"Vauban has organized entire districts into intrenched camps covered by streams, inundations, fortified towns, and forests, but he never contended that fortified cities alone could close the frontier."

~ "Notes on the Art of War," quoted in Jay Luvaas,
Napoleon on the Art of War, 1999

Napoleon observed that Sébastien Prestre de Vauban (1633–1707), the first great designer of military fortifications and perhaps the single most influential designer of forts in Western history, habitually integrated the features of the natural terrain into his systems of fortification, never arguing that artificial fortifications alone could close off a frontier to enemy attack and invasion.

Why reinvent the wheel? Begin all strategic planning with a survey of available resources. To the degree possible, integrate these into your plans. Effective and economical planning rarely begins from scratch.

■

Lesson 47
Ideal Plan versus Real World

> "In forming the plan of a campaign, it is requisite to foresee
> everything the enemy may do, and to be prepared with the nec-
> essary means to counteract it. Plans of campaign may be modi-
> fied, ad infinitum, according to circumstances—the genius of the
> general, the character of the troops, and the topography of the
> theater of action."
>
> ~Military Maxim II

Napoleon set a high standard for planning a campaign. His aim was
nothing less than to "foresee everything the enemy may do, and to
be prepared with the necessary means to counteract it." Yet he added
to this requirement the caveat that a campaign plan "may be modified, ad infinitum" to meet unfolding circumstances—that is, to cope
with the exigencies of the real world and accommodate life.

While Napoleon understood that a plan is the only weapon a
general has against the victory of mere chance, he also knew that all
plans were fragile and essentially doomed. The successful general
was for him one who formulated a great plan—and knew when to
modify or abandon it altogether.

A plan is a prediction. The most important components in the
execution of any plan are the awareness of when to depart
from it, the knowledge of how to depart from it, and the
strength of will to depart from or even discard it.

Lesson 48
Exercise Impulse Control

> "All wars should be governed by certain principles, for every war should have a definite object, and be conducted according to the rules of art. A war should only be undertaken with forces proportioned to the obstacles to be overcome."
>
> ~Military Maxim V

Few leaders of empire have been responsible for more wars in a briefer span of time than Napoleon, and yet he by no means undertook war lightly. Each campaign, each war had a definite object, and each—except for the bloated Russian campaign—was fought with armies exquisitely proportioned to the perceived scope of the objective. In terms of numbers, this usually meant that Napoleon's strength was significantly less than that of the enemy. But he understood that he enjoyed the advantage of forces that were better trained, more thoroughly committed, more cohesive, and far better led than those of the enemy. He generally fought with precision, employing just the number of troops he needed. It was only late in his career, when he yielded to the impulse of creating armies out of sheer numbers, sacrificing the quality of troops and officers to mere quantity, that he, his men, and his empire suffered. A major reason for the failure of the catastrophic Russian campaign of 1812 was his inability to support the vast army he led, which was made up largely of raw troops and was more rabble than disciplined military formation.

Embark boldly, but only after having planned carefully. If the objective of any contemplated initiative or program cannot be stated clearly in one to three grammatically correct sentences, the operation—absent some stroke of fortune—is doomed. Once your objective is clearly defined, proportion the required resources precisely. Overkill not only erodes the bottom line, it creates more problems than it solves.

Lesson 49
Don't Just Play the Game, Own It

> "Among mountains, a great number of positions are always to be found very strong in themselves, and . . . dangerous to attack. In mountain warfare, the assailant has always the disadvantage; even in offensive warfare in the open field, the great secret consists in defensive combats, and in obliging the enemy to attack."
>
> ~ Military Maxim XIV

Napoleon begins this maxim by formulating rules for attacking an enemy who occupies a naturally strong position in mountainous terrain. The approaches he proposes are all aimed at forcing the enemy to abandon the geographical advantages he enjoys. Napoleon ends by pointing out that, even "in the open field," a defender almost always enjoys advantages over an attacker, and that the "great secret" of victory in battle is not to attack but to oblige the enemy to attack you in your strongly defended, well-fortified position.

Napoleon's strategy and tactics were always as much about coaxing, luring, and forcing the enemy to relinquish advantages as they were about his own direct moves. He enjoyed the attack, but he believed it was even more effective to entice the enemy into a disadvantageous and costly attack on him. For Napoleon, victory almost always began by obliging the enemy to surrender as many of his options as possible. The lesson here is to gain control of your adversaries and competitors by putting them into positions that limit their options and allow you to run the table. Don't just play the game, own it.

Lesson 50
Do the Unexpected

> "The line of operation should not be abandoned; but it is one of the most skillful maneuvers in war, to know how to change it, when circumstances authorize or render this necessary. An army which changes skillfully its line of operation deceives the enemy, who becomes ignorant where to look for its rear, or upon what weak points it is assailable."
>
> ~Military Maxim XX

An army's "line of operation" is its route through the theater of war, from its starting point to its objective. Unlike many commanders, who advocated establishing multiple lines of operation, in the belief that redundancy created safety, Napoleon called for establishing just one line and then maintaining and defending it fiercely. He argued that multiple lines provided more vulnerability, not greater security. Obviously, a single line of operation made an attractive target for any enemy. Sever the line, and you could isolate an army as well as attack it from the rear. Equally obvious to an enemy was Napoleon's intention of defending his line of operation to the very last extremity. Because this seemed a certainty to his foes, Napoleon turned their assumption to his advantage; while ruling out abandoning the line, he proposed deliberately changing it as an important means of deceiving the enemy.

Napoleon's genius consisted in large part of his capacity for deception. He used the very principles of apparent certainty — the unquestioning assumptions he knew an adversary would make—as the foundation of his deceptions. Business generally puts a high premium on predictability and reliability. That is a given. For this very reason, a skilled leader and savvy competitor will, from time to time, do the unexpected. At times, deception and surprise are necessary to mislead an adversary, but even when you are not directly competing against another, taking an unexpected turn proclaims to colleagues and competitors alike that you are unique and irreplaceable.

■

Lesson 51
Have a Reason for Everything You Do

> "It should be laid down as a principle, never to have intervals by which the enemy can penetrate between corps formed in order of battle, unless it be to draw him into a snare."
>
> ~Military Maxim XXXIV

Napoleon did his best to reduce war to a set of rational principles, but he always allowed for the purposeful violation of his own rules. The only permission he required for breaking the rules was to have a good reason. Corps—the major constituent units of an army—were never to be spaced such that an enemy could get between them, *except* when there was a reason for doing so, namely a desire to lure the enemy into a trap.

Outside the realm of theory, principle must yield to judgment based on compelling reason. Never break a rule without a reason. But if you have a good reason, go ahead and break the rule.

■

Lesson 52
To Fight or to Settle?

"The keys of a fortress are well worth the retirement of the garrison, when it is resolved to yield only on those conditions. On
this principle it is always wiser to grant an honorable capitulation to a garrison which has made a vigorous resistance, than to
risk an assault."

~ Military Maxim XLVI

When he attacked a fortress, Napoleon's objective was almost
always to obtain the fortress, not to destroy its garrison. For this
reason, he was content to negotiate the capitulation of the fortress
and the withdrawal of the garrison rather than risk an assault—provided that the garrison had demonstrated a willingness to make "a
vigorous resistance."

Obtain your objective by the least costly, least risky means
available, even if compromise is required. Scale your aggression inversely to the perceived risk.

Lesson 53
Command Undivided

"Nothing is so important in war as an undivided command; for
this reason, when war is carried on against a single power, there
should be only one army, acting upon one base, and conducted by
one chief."

~ Military Maxim LXIV

Because Napoleon so frequently and vehemently proclaimed the
supremacy of an undivided command—a single general commanding a single unified army—it is easy to conclude that his

concept of leadership did not or could not contemplate multiple commanders leading divided forces. But read Military Maxim LXIV carefully, and you will note that the undivided command concept held only "when war is carried on against a single power." Napoleon had ample experience with wars conducted against multiple powers, and he developed a trusted cadre of marshals to lead armies against them variously, serially, or simultaneously, as the situation demanded.

The complexities of modern business, like the complexities of continental and even global warfare in Napoleon's time, rarely allow the luxury of a single commander leading a single army against a single adversary. Nevertheless, undivided command is still both possible and desirable. In planning a campaign, initiative, or project, divide areas of responsibility and phases of the operation, dedicating a single force under a single leader to each. The process must be coordinated, but if goals are efficiently analyzed and broken down into objectives, each objective can be obtained by a tightly choreographed unit led by a single manager. So effective is the principle of undivided command that investing the time and effort to design a project to enable it will almost always pay off in the quality of the final result.

■

Lesson 54
How to Evade Leadership

> "The same consequences which have uniformly attended long discussions and councils of war will follow at all times. They will terminate in the adoption of the worst course, which in war is always the most timid, or, if you will, the most prudent. The only true wisdom in a general is determined courage."
>
> ~ Military Maxim LXV

Napoleon did not eschew consultation or reject advice out of hand. Indeed, he gathered about him a distinguished coterie of scientists, scholars, and philosophers with whom he held long conversations. Nevertheless, he rigorously separated conversation and consultation from actual decision making, and for this reason he refused to honor the convention of his day, which called for a general to convene a council of war among his subordinate commanders before deciding on any course of action. Napoleon preferred to gather his military advice less formally. He often asked his subordinates pointed questions and even solicited their opinion. But the decision, when it came, was his and his alone.

Councils of war and other committees, in Napoleon's experience, never multiplied the boldness of their constituent commanders, but, on the contrary, multiplied fear, hesitation, caution, and timidity.

Not only was decision by committee an evasion of leadership, it tended to produce decisions aimed at avoiding defeat rather than achieving victory. "In war the general alone can judge of certain arrangements. It depends on him alone to conquer difficulties by his own superior talents and resolution." (Military Maxim LXVI)

Leadership by committee is an oxymoron. Any leader can benefit from multiple perspectives and advice prior to making a decision, but the decision itself must be the product of a single responsible mind. A committee decision almost always represents an evasion of leadership.

Lesson 55
Illusory Assets Are Real Liabilities

> "Had [Hannibal] left fortresses and depots in his rear he would
> have weakened his army."
> ~Napoleon, quoted in exile on St. Helena by his private secretary,
> Louis Antoine Fauvelet de Bourrienne, in R. W. Phipps, ed.,
> *Memoirs of Napoleon Bonaparte*, 1891

Napoleon marveled at Hannibal's epic march from Carthage into Europe, across the Ebro River, the Pyrenees, the Rhone, and, most famously, the Alps. "No more vast or extended plan has been executed by man," he remarked, judging Hannibal's expedition bolder than any expedition led by Alexander the Great.

Napoleon believed Alexander's march had been "wiser" than Hannibal's because he was careful to preserve communication between his advancing forces and the fortresses he established or the settlements he occupied and fortified, whereas Hannibal did no such thing. The Carthaginian took no steps to preserve communication with Spain or Carthage. In reading his musings on Hannibal, it is clear that this fact gave Napoleon pause. But, as he pondered the matter further, Napoleon realized that Hannibal's offensive war had been nevertheless "methodical" after all. "Had he left fortresses and depots in his rear he would have . . . compromised the success of his operations," Napoleon concluded. Depots and fortresses would have had to be garrisoned and defended, which would have required reducing the size of his offensive forces, thereby violating "Hannibal's principle [of keeping] his troops united." Had he violated this principle, Napoleon understood, he "would have been vulnerable everywhere." His offensive forces would have been smaller and therefore weaker, and his isolated garrisons would have been liable to attack from superior forces.

In the end, Napoleon observed, Hannibal did not wholly neglect communication with the rear; however, he left it to his few allies to establish and maintain. Fortresses and depots garrisoned by his own loyal troops might have provided Hannibal the feeling of greater safety, but a feeling of safety is not the same as safety. Such facilities would have been illusory assets but real liabilities.

> **Leverage and concentrate** your assets aggressively. Napoleon, like Hannibal, understood that the organization's precious resources had to be used to provide actual benefit, not the mere feeling of benefit. Illusory assets create real liabilities.

■

Lesson 56
The "Natural Principle"

> "All of these Great Captains of Antiquity . . . and those [who have] marched in their footsteps, have performed great deeds only by conforming to the rules and the natural principles of the art of war . . . the intelligent relationship between ends and means, and of efforts with obstacles."
> ~Napoleon, quoted in exile on St. Helena by his private secretary,
> Louis Antoine Fauvelet de Bourrienne, in R. W. Phipps, ed.,
> *Memoirs of Napoleon Bonaparte*, 1891

As his life wound down in exile on St. Helena, Napoleon confessed that his campaigns were dictated less by following "resolved plans" than by adherence to "general principles." Of these principles, the most essential—the "natural principle"—was the calculation of ends versus means. Napoleon saw this as the core principle of the art of war. It is also the master principle of business. As every decision relating to war was for Napoleon an equation of ends and means, so every decision relating to business must be one of reward versus risk, return versus investment, outcome versus effort. This is basic, and yet it is often obscured, neglected, or even lost sight of altogether. When this happens, managers begin to talk of "luck," a phenomenon Napoleon refused to associate with true leadership.

Plans come and go. "How many times," Napoleon mused at St. Helena, "have I been forced to completely change my plan?" But the successful leader nevertheless manages to find a still point, an unchanging principle that is her true north. Napoleon defined his still point as "the intelligent relationship between ends and means." Satisfy this principle, and you may make a good judgment or a bad one, but you will never abandon yourself to the drift of fortune. You will make, by definition, a principled decision.

■

Lesson 57
You Must Know Mathematics

> "To be a good general you must know mathematics; it serves to direct your thinking in a thousand circumstances."
> ~Napoleon, quoted in exile on St. Helena by his private secretary, Louis Antoine Fauvelet de Bourrienne, in R. W. Phipps, ed., *Memoirs of Napoleon Bonaparte*, 1891

Napoleon attached a number to virtually everything in war—tons of food, pairs of boots, depots of ammunition, enemy numbers versus his own—and calculated accordingly. He constantly quantified time, distance, and resources of all kinds.

It is no accident that his earliest military training was in the artillery, the most mathematical of the military sciences. And it was to this artillery background that Napoleon frequently attributed his success. He believed it necessary for every officer to serve time in the artillery, "which is the arm that can produce the most good generals."

To the degree that you can express a problem or an opportunity in numbers—time required, time saved, money required, money made—the odds of a correct decision and successful outcome increase greatly in your favor. Business runs on money, which is both the fuel and the product of intelligently applied effort; therefore, it is supremely important to quantify both effort and result in money made, spent, invested, saved, and lost.

3

Knowledge
and
Preparation

Lesson 58
Steep Yourself in Your Profession

> "When I had saved two écus of six livres I would hurry like a
> happy child to the bookstore."
>
> ~Recalling his cadet days, quoted in Robert Asprey,
> *The Rise of Napoleon Bonaparte,* 2000

Napoleon was a voracious reader throughout his life. As a penni-
less cadet, he "went often to look at the books [in bookstores]
with the sin of envy; I coveted [them] for a long time before my
purse allowed me to buy. Such were the joys and seductions of
my youth." He read philosophers from Plato to Rousseau, but he
was always drawn most intensely to the works of and about those
he would later dub history's "Great Captains." As a cadet, his
days were filled with soldiering and his nights with reading about
soldiering.

Think about your business every chance you get. Steep
yourself in your profession, which should occupy you in
reflection as well as in action. It should absorb your thinking
self as well as your doing self and seep into every corner of
your life.

■

Lesson 59
To Consult or Not to Consult

> "In military operations I consult nobody; in diplomatic operations I consult everybody."
>
> ~Letter to Citizen Letourneur, May 6, 1796

Napoleon realized that there was a place for both consultative leadership and absolute leadership, and that the only relevant issue was the ability to distinguish when one style or the other should be employed. He understood that military decisions were by their nature urgent, requiring the precision, clarity, and decisiveness that a solitary leader can deliver far more effectively than any committee. Diplomacy, he recognized, was a different matter, in which consultation with all concerned parties was essential to success.

> **As a decision maker,** one of the first decisions you should make is how to make decisions in a given sphere of activity. Consider emulating Napoleon by determining which areas require quick, decisive action best administered by you and you alone, and which areas either benefit from or absolutely demand consultation. There is no need to adopt a one-way-fits-all formula.

Lesson 60
To Your Health

> "In war good health is indispensable."
>
> ~Letter to the Minister of Foreign Relations, October 1, 1797

Ill health brings fatigue that distorts judgment, creates pessimism, and simply prevents a general from doing his job; "for it is at night when the commander must do his work," Napoleon wrote. Vigor not only enabled objective, clear-sighted decision making, it allowed the commander to be where he needed to be, which was, according to Napoleon, "everywhere." His advice was this: "A commander should not sleep."

Staying healthy is a leadership responsibility second to none. The job of creating and sustaining your organization is of necessity a marathon. Fail to care for your physical well-being, and you cannot go the distance.

Lesson 61
Take It All In

"Nothing [in Egypt] escaped [Napoleon's] observation . . . in a few weeks he was as well acquainted with the country as if he had lived in it for ten years."

~ Louis Antoine Fauvelet de Bourrienne,
Napoleon's personal secretary, 1798,
quoted in R. W. Phipps, ed.,
Memoirs of Napoleon Bonaparte, 1891

Those who saw Napoleon as nothing more than a conqueror interpreted the hungry look in his eyes as evidence of his unappeasable rapacity. There can be no denying that Napoleon was a man of—well—Napoleonic ambition. Yet his hungry look was less about his appetite for military conquest than it was an expression of his in-born and insatiable need to take in and comprehend all that he saw.

What Bourrienne said of him was hardly an original observation. Everyone who met Napoleon remarked on his intense curiosity and his eagerness to see and understand all. The man who would conquer the world possessed the ability to make himself at home anywhere in the world. In Egypt, he was accompanied by some of the most brilliant scientists and philosophers in France, and he also devoured books on Islam, which he came to understand intimately and in detail within a matter of weeks. Napoleon believed that this religion was the key to everything about Egyptian civilization, and he insisted that his officers learn about it and pay their respects to the native religion. Understanding, he believed, was a more permanent form of possession than conquest by mere force of arms.

> **Get curious** and stay curious. Observe the routines of your organization. Question how things are being done, including how you yourself are doing things. Make the new familiar while treating the familiar as if it were new. Rethink and revise what could be made to work better.

■

Lesson 62
Assume the Worst

> "I calculate on the basis of the worst possible case."
>
> ~Letter to the king of Naples, quoted in
> Felix Markham, *Napoleon*, 1963

Pessimism leads to defeatism. Napoleon was never a pessimist. On the contrary, he began every campaign imagining victory and the results of victory. Yet he made all of his hard calculations based on a worst-case scenario. "If I take so many precautions," he explained to the king of Naples, "it is because my custom is to leave nothing to chance."

We can only imagine the degree of self-discipline required for Napoleon to divorce his campaign planning and preparations from the natural optimism of the visionary conqueror that he was. Indeed, Napoleon confessed to "purposely exaggerate[ing] all the dangers and all the calamities that the circumstances make possible," such that, before a campaign, he was "in a thoroughly painful state of agitation." But he also made sure that his feelings did not prevent his "looking quite serene in front of [his] entourage," an endeavor he oddly compared to the situation of "an unmarried girl laboring with child."

Assuming the worst enabled Napoleon to plan carefully for all contingencies. The great secret of ensuring that this worst-case thinking did not poison the actual campaign was an ability to wall off his doubts (which he used as an aid to planning) from his optimism. In this way, he avoided sapping the sheer energy required to execute the plans. "Once I have made up my mind," he explained, "everything is forgotten except what leads to success."

■

Lesson 63
Take Notice of Those Who Hit the Most Targets

> "My intention is that in each regiment . . . notice will be taken of
> those gunners . . . who hit the most targets."
> ~Letter to General Louis-Alexandre Berthier, March 25, 1803

Napoleon directed his generals to appoint artillery inspectors to keep score during both gunnery practice and battle to determine which gunners hit the most targets and consistently fired most rapidly. In 1803, he ordered that from September 2 through 7, each regiment was to send those determined to be the best gunners to a specialized artillery school at La Fère, where they would be given intensive trial and training with every sort of gun and ammunition. Napoleon was interested not only in getting the ablest gunners but also in determining which of his regiments could most dependably supply the "best man who aims a gun." The point of the exercise was to create a steady supply of highly qualified artillerymen.

Identify your best employees. Find out where they come from. Ensure a reliable supply of your best. This is the essence of human resources management.

■

Lesson 64
Train Your Horses to Cross Rivers

"Regiments that are within reach of water [must] train their horses to cross rivers."

~Letter to General Louis-Alexandre Berthier, March 25, 1803

Armies don't cross rivers. Men do. Even more important during the nineteenth century and earlier, horses had to. Neglect this fact, and your army will be paralyzed by the merest stream.

A river is as formidable an obstacle as a mountain if you lack the means of crossing it. Napoleon understood that crossing a river is not in a horse's nature. He must be trained to it, and that training takes time and effort. When the need for maneuver in combat presents itself, it is already too late.

Determine what tools, knowledge, and skills you and your organization need. Now is the time to invest the resources and effort required to obtain and hone them. Load your toolbox with the tools you must bring to the job, then keep them razor sharp. Without the tools you need—when you really need them—nothing is possible.

■

Lesson 65
A Proper Reconnaissance

> "He will be accompanied by some Bavarian engineers but he will
> take care to see everything for himself."
> ~Instructions to General Henri-Gatien Bertrand, August 25, 1805

Napoleon deemed a "proper reconnaissance" the first prerequisite for victory. In a set of instructions for one of his generals drawn up in the summer of 1805, he specified of what just such a reconnaissance should consist. In the vicinity of the fortress at Passau, General Bertrand was to take note of the conditions of roads, the width of the river, the volume of water flowing, the "alternating domination of one or the other of the banks," the presence, number, and condition of ferryboats, bridges, and fords. Although he was to be accompanied by "Bavarian engineers," Napoleon specified that the general was to "take care to see everything for himself" and also to write down whatever the engineers could tell him about the conditions on the river. He was also to gather information from locals and other "very knowledgeable sources."

Napoleon's instructions to Bertrand continue in the same obsessive detail concerning location after location. The document does not make for very interesting reading, and to those who imagine Napoleon as a dashing military genius, a great improviser and charismatic leader, the document must be most disappointing. He comes across in it as a pedant, riveted by every detail. To those who have actually studied his military career, however, the instructions to Bertrand are vintage Napoleon. He was obsessive about the gathering of knowledge. The most incisive military historians have pointed to this quality as the key to his success. No one denies his skill as a strategist and tactician or his talent as a leader of men, but recent military scholarship suggests that his triumphs were due less to what he did during battle than to all that he did in preparing for battle. He made himself thoroughly familiar with the battleground, its terrain, its waterways, its weather, and its people. He mentally possessed a country before he ever set foot in it.

Napoleon had not read the ancient Chinese general and military theorist Sun Tzu, but he would have enthusiastically embraced his assertion that "Battles are won before a single bow is drawn." Napoleon fought out a battle in his mind—and not just the clash of armies, but also their routes of march, their means of sustenance and supply, their options for maneuver. He built his imagination of battle on the detailed information produced by firsthand, authoritative, and tediously detailed reconnaissance.

> **Bold, exciting action** for high stakes should be launched only from a solid platform of exhaustive knowledge. Never confuse the bluster of ignorance with the confidence born of thorough understanding.

■

Lesson 66
Get the Picture

> "Make a reconnaissance of Lake Majeur as far as the foot of Simplon, to determine if it can be crossed and also to have an accurate picture of it in your own mind."
>
> ~Letter to Eugène de Beauharnais,
> Prince Eugène, September 30, 1805

The Alps have figured as a formidable military obstacle since the days of Hannibal, and Napoleon, seeking to identify the most feasible means of negotiating this monumental terrain, asked his stepson, Prince Eugène, to make a reconnaissance. Napoleon specified two goals for this project. The first was to determine if Lake Maggiore (in French, *Majeur*) could be crossed as a means of access to the Simplon Pass through the Alps, and the second was for Eugène to develop an "accurate picture" *in his own mind* of the relation between the lake and the pass.

This was typical of Napoleon. He always conquered territory first and foremost in his own mind. He possessed the uncanny ability to effect a *coup d'oeil*—a "stroke of the eye"—by which he could read terrain and immediately evaluate its tactical advantages and disadvantages. It was precisely this quality that he wanted to develop in all of his generals, including his own stepson. Two-dimensional map knowledge, he knew, was insufficient to guide an army in its traversal of a territory or to show it how to fight and win a battle. Everything had to be envisioned in three dimensions—plus the fourth dimension of time—and he believed that a competent general had to possess the faculty of building such a picture in his mind both before and during a campaign. Moreover, he believed that, once the picture was acquired, it remained (as he wrote to Eugène) "in your mind for life"—becoming part of a great internal library for future victories and conquests.

A practical grasp of any complex strategic situation is never cursory, flat, or schematic, but fully visionary, offering a mental picture of reality in all possible dimensions of space, time, and circumstance. Building your grasp of a project, problem, or opportunity calls for an exercise of the imagination based on solid data, preferably gathered personally and at firsthand.

Lesson 67
Getting (Good) Advice

> "Never hold a council of war, but listen to the views of each in private."
> ~Letter to Joseph Bonaparte, January 12, 1806

Napoleon had his fill of both war making and government by committee early in his military career when he had to deal with the Directory, the council that led France during and immediately after the Revolution. Nevertheless, he did not close his eyes, ears, or mind to input from his generals; however, instead of taking the traditional step of convening a "council of war" before major decisions were made, he solicited the opinions and views of each commander privately and individually. Although he never discussed the advantages of this approach, we can guess them:

- Individual conferences promote originality in the assessment of the situation and issues under consideration.

- Individual conferences tend to ensure purity of opinion. Each officer would deliver his thoughts uncolored by those of others.

- Individual conferences tend to take ego posturing out of the equation. In councils of war, generals might try to impress one another or gain some advantage in the eyes of the chief.

- Individual conferences avoid the hazard of reaching consensus for the sake of consensus. The natural tendency of a committee is to produce agreement, not necessarily the best plan. By removing consensus as a goal of discussion, Napoleon ensured that he would be presented with a variety of ideas rather than a single synthetic idea. He could choose what was best among them.

• Although a committee may naturally work toward consensus, the process involves much arguing, which consumes time and effort and gets in the way of actually producing solutions. Napoleon was not interested in hearing arguments. He wanted ideas, which he and he alone would judge.

The approach Napoleon advised Joseph to take—obtaining counsel individually rather than in a group—discards any possibility of synergy in formulating tactics, strategy, procedures, and policies. Moreover, obtaining a clear consensus among the stakeholders in an enterprise promotes group ownership of the organization's programs and initiatives. Yet it is an approach worth pondering. We take for granted that committees, round tables, and group sessions are useful in generating ideas and providing multiple points of view. But, after the fifth group meeting in a week, what manager does not begin to wonder whether meetings have become the "real" business of the firm? The effort to build consensus can drive an organization or divert it. Napoleon advised an extreme solution. At the very least, his advice emphasizes the need for balance between the means and ends of the decision-making process. Action, not consensus, is the goal.

■

Lesson 68
Create the Conditions for Success

"Disarm the country: do it thoroughly."

~ Letter to Joseph Bonaparte, March 2, 1806

During the Spanish campaign, Napoleon advised his brother on steps to take to ensure the successful occupation of a conquered territory. He specified:

1. Disarm the country thoroughly.

2. Occupy the fortresses and turn the mortar batteries in them against the towns.

3. Arm and provision the captured fortresses so that any formation of soldiers could defend them against retaking by the populace.

4. Anticipate an insurrection "fifteen days sooner or later" following occupation. Napoleon not only counseled his brother not to fear an insurrection, but to treat it as an opportunity. He advised making harsh public examples of all who rise up. "As long as you have not made an example of anyone you will never be master." Anyone who stirs up rebellion "must be brought before a military tribunal and instantly shot. Two or three examples are indispensable, and must be made." Napoleon explained that he regarded an insurrection followed by harsh reprisal "in the same way as the father of a family looks upon smallpox in his children; provided it does not excessively weaken the inflicted, it is a beneficial crisis."

5. "Get rid of the prominent men; punish the smallest fault with severity."

6. Act benevolently after demonstrating your severity against troublemakers.

Napoleon never imposed his will on anyone without first creating conditions to make that imposition most effective. Increase the likelihood of success by creating a favorable environment. This may require public relations, special programs of education, provision of ombudsmen, special incentives, and so on.

■

Lesson 69
Create an Environment for Success

"Never lose sight of this maxim, that you should establish your cantonments at the most distant and best protected point from the enemy, especially where a surprise is possible. By this means you will have time to unite all your forces before he can attack you."

~ Military Maxim XXIV

Prudence and audacity are not incompatible. Napoleon believed that battles were won before a single shot was fired. He prepared carefully with the objective of creating the circumstances that would ensure his success. Whereas some commanders would establish cantonments (temporary encampments) as close as possible to the battlefield to shorten the march to combat, Napoleon enlisted distance as an ally, setting up his encampments at a sufficient distance from the enemy to give him the time and space in which to maneuver, unite, and concentrate his forces where and when they were needed to repel the enemy.

Be prudent in preparation but bold in execution. Success begins before the project is launched. A hundred factors can doom any endeavor, beginning with your own failure to create an environment in which triumph is the most likely outcome.

■

Lesson 70
The Only Information Is Precise Information

"I must have precise information to adjust my movement and formulate my plan."

~Letter to Eugène de Beauharnais, Prince Eugène, March 24, 1806

General Patton jotted in his field notebook, "The only discipline is perfect discipline." Napoleon might have declared something similar about information: *The only information is precise information*. He defined "precise information" in a letter to his stepson, Prince Eugène, as "detailed information," including such items as the width and length of islands, the elevation of mountains, the width of canals, "the nature of fortified cities, fortress by fortress," and the condition of available roads.

Although information was for Napoleon the most valuable of all commodities, he believed that torturing men to gain their secrets was counterproductive, producing "nothing worthwhile." The word of spies he likewise rejected as untrustworthy. Only by intensively studying the country in which the battles are fought does a commander gain the precise knowledge he needs. "Local knowledge is precious knowledge," Napoleon wrote.

> **Information gathered at** first hand by and from those with intimate knowledge of "local" (that is relevant) conditions is, by definition, precise information—the only information Napoleon and other successful leader-planners accept as actionable.

■

Lesson 71

Safety Last

> "And none will have any defensive arms."
>
> ~ "Project for the New Organization of the Army," quoted
> in Jay Luvaas, *Napoleon on the Art of War*, 1999

Light cavalry—including hussars (mainly skirmishers) and chasseurs ("hunters" trained and equipped for very rapid action)—were the shock troops of Napoleon's armies. They formed the advance guard and were intended to be the first units to make contact with the enemy.

Above all else, Napoleon wanted two things from his light cavalry. The first was utmost mobility; the second, utmost offensive aggressiveness. To promote the first quality, he prescribed arming these troopers with an extremely light carbine and bayonet, together weighing under six pounds—less than half the weight of a standard infantry musket. Each cavalryman would also be issued a pair of pistols, designed to hang from the saddle and each weighing less than a pound. The sabers for these units would weigh no more than three pounds. Half the troopers would also be equipped with lances.

All of the weapons Napoleon prescribed for his light cavalrymen ensured their absolute offensive orientation. Not only would these shock troops be issued offensive weapons, they would not be issued or even be permitted to carry "any defensive arms."

Was there a risk in providing no long-range muskets or heavy sabers—the customary means of defense? Perhaps. But Napoleon reasoned that the greater risk lay in giving these troopers the equipment to choose a defensive rather than an offensive posture. By denying them the equipment of defense, Napoleon sought to compel them to act aggressively at all times. Indeed, he even prescribed "simple, large, and comfortable" uniforms because he expected light cavalry troopers to "sleep fully clothed, in peacetime as well as in war." There would be no rest, nothing savoring of garrison life. The light cavalrymen would be equipped for maximum combat readiness and for nothing else at all times.

> **Provide your team** with what it needs to do the job you *want* it to do, not the job you *don't* want it to do. If, for example, you want Workgroup A to prospect for new clients and Workgroup B to develop more business with established clients, supply Workgroup A with leads, research, and other tools necessary to find new customers. Do not provide them with a database of established customers. Give that to Workgroup B, and instruct them to work that database and that database only. The right equipment—with nothing extra—promotes the productive intensity that keeps your workgroups focused on their missions.

■

Lesson 72
Your Big Guns

> "Only with cannon can one wage war."
> ~ Letter to General Jean-Baptiste Jules Bernadotte,
> February 27, 1807

For Napoleon, artillery was the sovereign weapon of war. With it "great battles are won," and while (he conceded) it "may be true that good infantry is the nerve of the army, . . . if it has to fight for long against superior artillery it [will] become demoralized and be destroyed." Napoleon pointed out the reality that, no matter how brave, infantry cannot "march 3,000 or 3,600 feet with impunity against sixteen or twenty-four well-placed guns, served by good gunners."

If artillery was both indispensable and omnipotent, it was also burdensome. Preparing the artillery, Napoleon pointed out, takes much more time than preparing either infantry or cavalry. "It is always the artillery that holds up the formation of armies."

Thus, as with heavy cavalry, the greatest potential asset of an army is also its greatest potential liability. To ensure that his artillery always functions as an asset, the general must prepare well in advance. Napoleon left as little to chance as possible. He created what he called "my system of regular war," which dictated a "large quantity of artillery"—at least as much as the enemy and more precisely quantified as "four guns per 1,000 infantry and cavalry." Each gun was required to travel with 300 rounds of ammunition, which Napoleon calculated as the "normal expenditure for two battles."

> **No weapon,** no tool, no asset plans itself, prepares itself, operates itself, or pays for itself. Without adequate planning and intelligent management, every asset becomes at the very least a burden and at the worst a liability. The more powerful the tool, the more valuable the asset, the greater the challenge to leadership.

■

Lesson 73
Dig for the Details

"I expected several pages and I get only two lines."
~Letter to General Henri-Gatien Bertrand, March 4, 1807

"Your letter tells me nothing," Napoleon wrote in disgust to Henri-Gatien Bertrand, one of his most trusted lieutenants. He was disappointed by the cursory report Bertrand had provided on conditions in and about Danzig, which was to be the object of a siege (beginning March 18) in the War of the Fourth Coalition. Napoleon wanted Bertrand to furnish the names of the enemy regiments, the names of their commanding generals, and "a hundred things, all very important," including the morale of the enemy, how they are fed, the strength of

various units, and "what is known from conversations with colonels and officers of the corps." This, Napoleon chided, should have filled several pages, not the two meager lines he had been sent. "Redeem all that by writing me in great detail."

Too many managers live and die by the "executive summary." Such documents are to the reality of a situation what a one-page outline of Shakespeare's *Hamlet* is to the play itself. Summaries and once-overs kill rather than create practical, effective understanding. Their effect is the more insidious because they give the illusion of mastery when there is none. There is no shortcut to building a grasp of the truly important, high-stakes opportunities and problems. Detailed, dependable, and nuanced information is called for, and it must be examined and digested personally. Anything less is reliance on illusion.

■

Lesson 74
Vive la Différence

"Three fourths of the people . . . have no idea at all of the differences among troops."

~Letter to Joseph Bonaparte, October 18, 1807

To some generals, troops are troops. To Napoleon, they were human resources of varying and distinct skills and value, which he made it his business to know and understand. He wrote to his brother that Swiss soldiers were notable for bravery, fidelity, and loyalty, so he decided that the Swiss regiments he employed would consist exclusively of "Swiss citizens without any mixture of deserters or other foreigners." Russian troops he considered brave, but less so than French; moreover, they tended to be ignorant and sluggish, making Russian armies "less formidable" than French armies. The Poles, in contrast, were the

"French of the north," whereas German troops were inferior to Russian, and Italian troops inferior to German. For this reason, he believed it a bad practice to mix Italian and French soldiers in the same units. Worst of all, Napoleon claimed, were Westphalian soldiers.

The point here is not to recognize some early form of ethnic stereotyping or racial profiling, but to understand that Napoleon saw an army in more dimensions than just its numbers. Far more important was the quality, motivation, and character of the troops. He believed it a grave error to create "colonial battalions," explaining to Joseph that "putting arms in the hands of wretched subjects is a fatal [notion]." Conscripts might be a necessary evil in an army, but "refractory conscripts" should not be assigned to service in branches that require a high level of skill and commitment, such as the artillery, sappers (the advance guard), and cavalry. Napoleon also thought mixing men of many nations in a single army was a serious error. "Greeks in the service of Alexander the Great felt no passion for the cause," he pointed out. One could compensate somewhat for a deficiency of passion by providing good leadership, good organization, and good discipline, but "fanaticism, love of country, and national glory can better inspire young soldiers."

It is a common mistake to throw people at a project or a problem. As Napoleon counseled his brother Joseph, it is "not large numbers of troops that you must apply yourself to have, but a small number of good troops that you can train progressively." Recruit employees and team members for their general qualities and for the specific qualifications you need. Learn to distinguish among candidates, and put the highest value on those you can train, mentor, and develop as precisely the kind of problem solvers you need. The true art of managing human resources is to create value through leveraged efficiency, building an organization that can do the best with the least.

Lesson 75
History? Don't Try to Escape It

> "Histories of wars are filled with too many illustrious catastrophes
> for us to hasten to get into a scrape in the narrow city streets."
>
> ~ "Notes on the Actual Position of the Army in Spain,
> July 21, 1808," quoted in Jay Luvaas, *Napoleon on the Art of War*, 1999

Napoleon well understood that to lose the ability to maneuver is to lose the battle. For him, the ideal battlefield met two criteria:

1. It was of his choosing, not the enemy's.

2. It allowed him to maneuver to create an envelopment, holding the enemy with a small force on the front while attacking with his main units on a flank and rear.

An urban landscape provided no room for maneuver and therefore gave all the advantages to the defenders, who could fire from the covered and concealed heights of buildings and create murderous crossfire along streets so narrow as to reduce a march to a crawl while also preventing volley fire from a rank formation.

Napoleon's own military imagination and common sense would have been sufficient to warn him away from cities, but when he wanted to convey this insight to the generals fighting the war in Spain during 1808 (a battlefront he left in charge of his subordinates, with catastrophic results), he did not rely on his own instinct, but on history. He cited in particular the recent Second Battle of Buenos Aires (1807), in which British lieutenant general John Whitelocke left half his force dead on the urban battlefield and, on his return to England, was court-martialed and relieved of command. Even for Napoleon, who prided himself on making his own history, the lessons of the history of others were powerful guides, alerting him to dangers as well as opportunities.

Here is Napoleon's relationship with history: Refusing to be trapped by it, he nevertheless studied it avidly, assiduously mining the many lessons it offered.

Lesson 76

In War Everything Is Mental

"Exaggerate."

~Letter to General Henri-Jacques-Guillaume Clarke,

October 10, 1809

Napoleon made his brother Joseph king of Spain and, as a result, had nothing but trouble from that corner of the world thereafter. Either directly or through others, he found himself continually instructing "His Majesty." When Joseph was foolish enough to pub-lish figures on the strength of his armies in Spain, Napoleon asked General Clarke to convey to him that, in the future, whenever he might be "induced to reveal the strength of his forces," he should "exaggerate . . . by doubling or trebling the number," and that, whenever he mentioned the enemy, he should diminish the enemy's force "by half or one third."

"In war," Napoleon declared to General Clarke, "everything is mental." Napoleon explained that "Man is naturally inclined to believe" in the absolute and inevitable rule of numbers, that greater numbers will always defeat lesser numbers. Therefore, while there is great advantage in making your side believe it outnumbers the enemy, there is no advantage in their believing themselves outnum-bered—even if that is the truth. Moreover, Napoleon also discerned a "natural instinct" to "see the enemy as . . . larger in numbers than he actually is." This made it even more imperative to exaggerate one's own strength.

"In war, intellect and judgment are the better part of reality," Napoleon wrote to Clarke. The "Great Captains" of history, he explained, have been those who have made "their own forces appear to be very large to the enemy and to make the enemy view them-selves as being very inferior." Napoleon, especially in his early campaigns, achieved this deception repeatedly.

Since the days of Socrates and Plato, *What is reality?* has been the most basic question of philosophy. Napoleon was confident he had the answer, at least in war. This master of roads, rivers, and mountains, of guns, horses, and men—of all the physical elements of armed engagement—knew that the *real* "reality" existed within those who plan, lead, and fight. He did not deny the physical facts of warfare, but they melted away before perception, fear, confidence, imagination, and vision.

Look away from the spreadsheet flickering on the screen before you. Look inside your own head. Take inventory *there*. Create *there* what you need to win. Then, share that mental reality with your entire enterprise.

■

Lesson 77

The Fatal Mix

"The mixture of good and bad portions is fatal—worse than if all the parts were bad."

~ Letter to General Henri-Jacques-Guillaume Clarke,
December 19, 1809

After examining a map of Germany he had commissioned, Napoleon angrily ordered it sent back—not because it was all bad, but because it was a mixture of good and bad, which he considered worse than if it were uniformly bad.

"When it comes to maps," he wrote to General Clarke, "we must have only good ones, or else the dubious or poor sections must be colored to indicate that one should not trust them."

In all mission-critical work, it is essential to know what you know and also to know what you do not know. Obviously bad information can be rejected out of hand, but more subtly tainted data is an ambush, inviting decisions and actions that may prove fatal. While every effort must be made to obtain the best intelligence, it is also true that the best should not be allowed to become an enemy of the good. Dubious or incomplete intelligence is better than none—*provided that* those acting on the data have the tools to separate the good portions from the bad. If these tools are unavailable, all of the intelligence should be rejected.

■

Lesson 78
Convert the Essential to Second Nature

> "Acquaint them with the theory and explain it to them every day
> so that this . . . becomes second nature to them."
> ~Letter to Marshal Auguste-Frédéric-Louis Marmont,
> April 17, 1813

In Napoleon's day, the most basic, effective, and essential defensive maneuver available to infantry units under attack by cavalry was the infantry—or "hollow"—square. It worked like this:

When attacked, an infantry battalion (500 to 1,000 men) would rapidly form itself into a square or rectangle, each side of which was composed of at least two ranks of soldiers armed with muskets or rifles, bayonets fixed. The battalion commander would take a position at the center of the square, along with the unit's colors and a reserve force he could send to reinforce any side of the square that looked to be in danger of breaking under the attack.

As the attackers approached, the defending troops would fire volleys at them, one rank firing while the other reloaded and prepared to fire. A skilled and courageous commander would order fire to be held until the charging cavalry was less than a hundred feet from the square. This greatly increased the accuracy of the defensive fire, piling up dead and wounded men and horses between the square and the attackers, thereby further impeding the attack.

The infantry square was a very effective 360-degree defense, provided that it could be formed quickly and accurately and assuming that the defensive fire was highly disciplined, rapid, and accurate. With a body of fast-charging horses and riders bearing down on you, such efficiency of movement and discipline of fire were not easy to achieve. Panic was the attacker's ally. Panic would undermine discipline, rendering the defensive fire much less accurate and leaving soldiers with empty muskets even as the attackers closed in. Therefore, Napoleon stressed the vital importance of making the infantry square "second nature" to the officers responsible for forming it. His prescription was to instill in each officer a full understanding of the theory behind the infantry square. This was drilled into the officers daily so that, in commanding the square, they would do much more than go through rote motions. Napoleon sought to achieve a quick, natural, and *intelligent* understanding of the elements of the art of war among his subordinates in the field. While he wanted to be able to count on a reliable response, he was far less interested in eliciting blind obedience than in encouraging creative, active action that conformed to his overall plan.

Napoleon's military leadership style more closely resembles management theory appropriate to most modern "flat" organizational structures (in which authority and information are widely shared among teams and individuals) than it does traditional hierarchical management structures (in which authority and information are held at the top and trickled down in miserly fashion, as deemed necessary). Information is power, and the modern leader-manager believes (as Napoleon did) that knowledge shared widely within the enterprise is more powerful than power hoarded at the top.

Lesson 79
Too Much Is Not Enough

> "The greatest defect in general administration is to want to do too
> much: that results in not having what is needed."
> ~Letter to Baron de Saint-Aignan, April 20, 1813

In a letter to his ambassador to Weimar, the Baron de Saint-Aignan, Napoleon criticized the mapmaker engineers whose responsibility it had been to draw up a set of operational battle maps. He described them as "too much masters of what they wish to do." It was a characteristic, he explained, that drove them to attempt to create in the maps something far more elaborate than he had asked for. The result of this overreaching was a failure to deliver "what is needed," namely a map indicating nothing more or less than roads and mountain passes that either could or could not be negotiated by armies with artillery.

Information, to be useful—to be "actionable"—must be accurate, detailed, and relevant. Over-delivering data is counterproductive because the excess obscures the essential. While a shortage of information is undesirable, an overabundance of information is just as destructive to creating and maintaining a picture of the reality of a particular situation. For purposes of waging war, Napoleon needed very specific kinds of information rendered with absolute clarity. This required gathering some kinds of data and rejecting others to create only the necessary picture.

Information overload—the over-delivery of data—flattens the picture of a given situation and diminishes rather than enhances understanding. Endeavor to provide information economically, furnishing just enough to enable accurate and effective action. When asked for data, tailor your response to the request rather than to the measure of your own opinions, ambitions, and desires.

■

Lesson 80
Logistics by Prescription

> "Every five or six marches you must have a fortified city or entrenched position . . . where you can assemble the magazines for victuals and military supplies, organized convoys, and which you can make the center of maneuver, a pivot mark that shortens the line of operations."
>
> ~Order of the Day, May 12, 1813

Logistics is the least glamorous aspect of war, but it is so important that Napoleon declared that, "according to the laws of war, the general who loses his line of operations deserves death."

Because logistics is about quantities and consumption, it naturally lends itself to prescriptive planning. A general knows the size of his army, and he knows how much food and ammunition each soldier needs; therefore, he may readily calculate his logistical requirements. Figure in the dimensions of time and distance, and creating a formula for the placement of depots and fortifications—supply points—becomes a rational process. Napoleon expressed the need for such facilities in terms of the number of marches (1 march equals 1 day) between them.

Be grateful for those aspects of tactical and strategic planning that can be readily quantified. Each prescription you can write removes one more unknown from your plan and frees you up for coping with the less predictable and the utterly unforeseeable.

■

Lesson 81
Quantify Your Advantages and Liabilities

"Two Mamelukes would keep three Frenchmen at bay."

~ "Notes on the Art of War," quoted in Jay Luvaas,

Napoleon on the Art of War, 1999

Those who enjoy consistent success playing the horses are the first to tell you: *Winning bettors never gamble.* If you want to make money on horse races, you'd better learn to be a super-capable handicapper—someone with the judgment and know-how to quantify the advantages and liabilities of each animal at the starting gate.

Napoleon was a brilliant handicapper when it came to evaluating the odds of one army's prevailing against another. He never relied on gut instinct, but always endeavored to quantify advantages and liabilities.

Napoleon's mathematical orientation was very much in evidence during the Egyptian campaign, during which he proposed the following calculations: two Mamelukes (members of an elite Egyptian military caste) could, he predicted, "keep three Frenchman at bay because they are better armed, better mounted, better drilled . . . have several horses, and several footmen to serve them." But when French cavalry operated in larger numbers, the superiority of French tactics counteracted the Mamelukes' individual advantages, such that 100 French cavalrymen had no need to fear 100 Mamelukes, 300 French troopers need not fear 400 Mamelukes, and 600 should not be afraid of 900.

Napoleon constantly sought to replace prediction based on guesswork and hunches with prediction based on precise quantification. For him, numbers enforced an intellectual discipline that made evaluation of even the most fluid situations more reliable, more comprehensible, and more likely to produce positive results.

Calculus is a mathematical discipline intended to reduce multiple variables to order and some degree of certainty. Napoleon consistently applied a kind of calculus to the chaos of combat. The more a manager can employ the objectifying scale of quantity—of numbers—the greater the rationality of her decisions concerning risk versus reward. Create a calculus that works for you. The more effectively you can handicap your bets, the less you operate as a gambler and the more you become the true leader of your enterprise.

■

Lesson 82
Evaluate the Obstacle

> "The frontiers of states are either large rivers, or chains of mountains, or deserts. Of all these obstacles to the march of an army, the most difficult to overcome is the desert; mountains come next, and broad rivers occupy the third place."
>
> ~Military Maxim I

Napoleon was intimately familiar with natural obstacles. Each presented a unique difficulty, and he made it his business to learn just how each could be conquered. He did not lump them together, but carefully discriminated among them, rating their difficulty.

Most revelatory, perhaps, is rating the desert a more difficult obstacle than mountains. Common sense would suggest that mountains should claim the first place, but Napoleon based his evaluation on experience—the Egyptian campaign—and not common sense. In any case, the bottom line is that he rated none of the three major natural obstacles as "impossible."

Do not turn away from obstacles. Understand them. Evaluate them. Learn about them from experience—yours and that of others. Start from the assumption that all obstacles can be overcome.

■

Lesson 83
Know What It Means to Be Ready

"An army should be ready every day, every night and at all times of the day and night, to oppose all the resistance of which it is capable. With this view, the soldier should always be furnished completely . . . and the different divisions of the army should be constantly in a state to support, to be supported, and to protect itself.

"The troops, whether halted, or encamped, or on the march, should be always in favorable positions, possessing the essentials required for a field of battle."

~ Military Maxim VII

Napoleon declared that an army should always be ready. Who could doubt the wisdom of this maxim? But, being a practical leader, he went on to demonstrate his knowledge of precisely what it means to be ready.

• Everyone must be properly equipped.

• All elements of the organization must be prepared to function properly together and to support one another.

• All elements of the organization must be positioned to be available and effective in the shortest possible time.

• All elements of the organization must be positioned for maximum efficiency.

It is easy to say, "Be prepared," but this resolution means nothing unless you understand what comprises preparedness. In addition to planning specific projects and initiatives, prepare a plan for the times in between one project and the next. Formulate what you need in order to be prepared to take advantage of opportunities and overcome problems promptly and efficiently. Equip your organization accordingly, and be certain everyone is poised for action. Planning a rapid transition from down time to maximum effort is as important as planning the effort itself.

■

Lesson 84
Never Sacrifice Coordination

"To direct operations with lines far removed from each other, and without communications, is to commit a fault which always gives birth to a second. The detached column has only its orders for the first day. Its operations on the following day depend upon what may have happened to the main body. Thus this column either loses time upon emergency, in waiting for orders, or it will act without them, and at hazard. . . . [A]n army should always keep its columns so united as to prevent the enemy from passing between them with impunity. . . . [A]nd every precaution should be taken to prevent an attack upon them in detail."

~ Military Maxim XI

On a strategic level, Napoleon's ambitions were broad—even global—but, tactically, he was always a believer in concentration, consolidation, and close coordination. His preference was always to keep his forces united, if not in one continuous line of battle, then at least connected by an unbroken line of communications. His purpose was to avoid obliging the detached corps to waste time waiting for operational orders from the main body of the army or, even worse, to take independent action uncoordinated with the rest of the army.

Although Napoleon set up the maintenance of communication as a primary operational requirement, he recognized that, "for particular reasons," the principle of unity might have to be violated. When this was the case, he specified that the commanders of the detached corps be granted explicit permission to give orders independently, albeit with the single object of continually advancing toward a point established for uniting with the rest of the army or with other corps. In this way, the detached corps would not be idle while awaiting orders or guess about the correct action to take.

The actions of every component in an enterprise must contribute to the overall objectives and goals of the enterprise; therefore, create systems necessary to enable coordinated action among all units of the organization. This said, also provide for accidental breakdown in communications or purposeful departure from coordination by creating policies for independent action by subordinate leaders under a specific set of circumstances. These plans and policies must be in place before they are needed.

■

Lesson 85
Banish the Arbitrary

> "The distances permitted between [the] corps of an army upon
> the march must be governed by the localities, by circumstances,
> and by the object in view."
>
> ~ Military Maxim XIII

War, Napoleon was the first to admit, is subject to many variables that are difficult if not impossible to predict. His object in both planning and execution was to replace the random elements as much as possible with calculated certainty. This meant that nothing about an operation or a march should be determined arbitrarily—including arbitrary adherence to prescriptions and traditions. Instead of prescribing a permitted distance between marching corps, Napoleon offered a dynamic formula based on the realities of the given situation.

Uncertainty cannot be resolved with arbitrary rules and prescriptions. The most effective, most rational policies are responsive to actual rather than predicted or preconceived conditions. The most effective rules and prescriptions are those that guide the most efficient responses to reality.

■

Lesson 86
Determine Root Qualities

> "The first qualification of a soldier is fortitude under fatigue and privation. Courage is only the second; hardship, poverty, and want are the best school for the soldier."
>
> ~Military Maxim LVIII

Although Napoleon held that "a love of country, a spirit of enthusiasm, a sense of national honor, and fanaticism will operate upon young soldiers with advantage" (Military Maxim LVI), he believed the root of good soldiering ran deeper, simpler, and plainer. "Fortitude under fatigue and privation" seemed to him the "first qualification" of a soldier. Far from the elevated sentiments of patriotism and the romantic hunger for glory, these homely, hard, and decidedly unglamorous qualities were what he sought.

In recruiting a team, decide precisely what qualities the work demands. Be prepared to look through or beyond theory, mythology, and hype to match the nature of the job with the orientation and skill set of the individuals who are expected to do it. Consider especially the root qualities the position calls for, which are created by a mix of background, professional experience, personal character, and attitude. Unlike the superficial qualifications generally found in job descriptions, they are not readily learned, but are the transferable values an employee brings to a position. They are what you are paying for and investing in.

■

Lesson 87
Decide on the Basic Tools

> "There are five things the soldier should never be without—his musket, his ammunition, his knapsack, his provisions (for at least four days), and his entrenching tool. The knapsack may be reduced to the smallest size possible, if it be thought proper, but the soldier should always have it with him."
>
> ~Military Maxim LIX

As Napoleon saw it, equipping the individual soldier was a matter of providing all the right equipment without overburdening either the man or the treasury. He whittled the essentials down to just five basics: musket, ammunition, knapsack, four days' provisions, and an entrenching tool. Without musket and ammunition, the soldier cannot perform his principal task, which is fighting. Without a knapsack and provisions, he cannot shelter and sustain himself. Without an entrenching tool, he can neither dig a latrine nor a firing hole from which to defend a position. Each tool was essential on a daily or nearly daily basis. None would be dead weight or an unnecessary expense. The absence of any would render the soldier less effective, perhaps ineffective, and would therefore work against achieving victory.

Provide yourself and those you lead with what is needed to do the job. The most effective means of determining what is essential is to imagine each position without certain equipment. For example, an office-based customer service rep can do without a smartphone furnished on the company dime, but a technician in the field almost certainly cannot. Cut corners, and you reduce the efficiency and effectiveness of your workforce. Provide too much, and you not only waste resources on equipment and services, you burden people with equipment they do not need. Assembling the right toolkit may require actively analyzing the nature of the mission and the job rather than relying on assumptions or standardized prescriptions.

Lesson 88
Consider the Source

> "All the information obtained from prisoners should be received with caution. . . . A soldier seldom sees anything beyond his company; and an officer can afford intelligence of little more than the position and movements of the division to which his regiment belongs. On this account the general of an army should never depend upon the information derived from prisoners, unless it agrees with the reports received from the advanced guards."
>
> ~Military Maxim LXIII

Napoleon was always hungry for intelligence, but he consumed it with the sophistication of a gourmet, not the indiscriminate lust of the gourmand. Napoleon concluded that too many of his commanders accepted whatever prisoners told them uncritically. The results were usually unreliable, not because the prisoners consciously set out to deceive, but because lower-level enlisted men and officers had only a narrow and partial view of the combat situation. Their vision was limited in scope to their own unit and, in the case of officers, perhaps one echelon above their unit. Napoleon therefore counseled carefully corroborating whatever intelligence was derived from prisoner interrogation. Such corroboration could be obtained from one's own advance guard, which actually had the best view of the enemy's positions.

All data is not created equal. Its content, slant, spin, and value cannot be divorced from its origin. In evaluating data, always consider its source and adjust your interpretation accordingly. Perspective is everything.

■

Lesson 89
Be a Jack of All Trades and a Master of One

> "The commandant of artillery should understand well the general principles of each branch of the service, since he is called upon to supply arms and ammunition to the different corps. . . . His correspondence with the commanding officers of artillery at the advanced posts should put him in possession of all the movements of the army, and the disposition and management of the great park [main position] of artillery should depend upon this information."
>
> ~Military Maxim LXXV

The function of artillery in Napoleon's armies was to support the other two principal combat arms, the infantry and the cavalry; therefore, Napoleon required that artillery commanders know more than the art and science of their combat arm and also possess a firm understanding of the requirements of the arms they must support. Without this understanding, the artillery commander would be unable to function adequately in coordination with infantry and cavalry. Moreover, because artillery could not be moved quickly but had to be positioned optimally from the outset of battle, the artillery commander was also required to comprehend the big picture of the disposition and movement of all troops.

The leaders and managers of any enterprise should, like Napoleon's artillery commander, be experts in their specialty but also possess a sufficient understanding of all aspects of the organization to ensure that their decisions take into account the needs, limitations, and potential of all units and individuals. A leader must not allow her particular training and experience to prompt her to favor one department or phase of the operation over another. Every leadership decision must contemplate and encompass the productivity and welfare of the whole organization.

Lesson 90
Obtain Intelligence in All Dimensions

> "The qualities which distinguish a good general of advanced posts
> are: to reconnoiter accurately defiles and fords of every description;
> to provide guides that may be depended on; to interrogate the curé
> and postmaster; to establish rapidly a good understanding with the
> inhabitants; to send out spies; to intercept [translate, and analyze]
> letters; in a word, to be able to answer every question of the general-
> in-chief when he arrives with the whole army."
>
> ~Military Maxim LXXVI

Napoleon's definition of useful–usable–advance intelligence was
simple: it "answer[s] every question of the general-in-chief when he
arrives with the whole army." His description of just what goes into such
vital question-answering intelligence was more detailed and ranged
from the physical scouting of the places through which an army can
enter and exit but which may expose it to fire and ambush ("defiles"), to
river crossings ("fords"), to what modern experts call "human
intelligence"–information gathered through conversation, interrogation,
surveillance, and espionage. In short, Napoleon demanded multidimensional intelligence to guide his major operations.

Multidimensional intelligence answers questions in depth
and from a variety of sources, which act to corroborate and
correct one another. Napoleon emphasized gathering multidimensional intelligence firsthand, and he eschewed reliance on
rumor or single sources.

Business today is flooded with information. We swim in it,
sometimes carried along by the prevailing current, sometimes
struggling against it, too often on the verge of being drowned
by it. In an effort to use information before it is available to
competitors—"discounted into the market"—we are often
tempted to act on hint, rumor, and mere impression instead of

multidimensional intelligence. While delay in acting to correct a problem or exploit an opportunity can mean a loss, time invested in acquiring information of depth and quality is far more likely to prevent loss and ensure success.

■

Lesson 91
Rely Entirely on Yourself (with a Little Help from History)

> "Generals-in-chief must be guided by their own experience, or their genius. Tactics, evolutions, the duties and knowledge of an engineer or artillery officer may be learned in treatises, but the science of strategy is only to be acquired by experience, and by studying the campaigns of all the great captains.

> "Gustavus Adolphus, Turenne, and Frederick, as well as Alexander, Hannibal, and Caesar have all acted upon the same principles. These have been–to keep their forces united; to leave no weak part unguarded; to seize with rapidity on important points.

> "Such are the principles which lead to victory, and which, by inspiring terror at the reputation of your arms, will at once maintain fidelity and secure subjection."
>
> ~Military Maxim LXXVII

Strategic genius, according to Napoleon, could not be acquired from books in the way that the basics of military engineering and artillery could be. The only guide to the creation of victorious strategy was a general's own experience, combined with his "genius" and informed by "studying the campaigns of all the great captains." What is more, as Military Maxim LXXVII implies, it was not slavish imitation of the "Great Captains" that was called for, but an understanding of the principles that underlay their campaigns. Having thoroughly internalized these principles, Napoleon enumerated them in his military maxim:

1. Keep forces united.

2. Leave no weak point unguarded.

3. Determine the objectives that must be seized, and seize them rapidly.

Decipher the connections between the great campaigns of history and these principles, Napoleon's advice implies, and you will not only achieve victory but also will acquire a reputation that will "inspire terror" and thus "at once maintain fidelity and secure subjection."

As he elaborated in Military Maxim LXXVIII: "Peruse again and again the campaigns of Alexander, Hannibal, Caesar, Gustavus Adolphus, Turenne, Eugene [Prince Eugene of Savoy (1663–1736), one of the most spectacularly successful and prolific commanders in European military history], and Frederick. Model yourself upon them. This is the only means of becoming a great captain and of acquiring the secret of the art of war. Your own genius will be enlightened and improved by this study, and you will learn to reject all maxims foreign to the principles of these great commanders."

There is no excuse for the failure of a CEO or manager to acquire a working knowledge of all major operational phases of the organization she leads; however, technical knowledge is no substitute for strategic thinking based on experience informed by the "best practices" of others. In the end, as a leader, you must rely entirely on yourself—with a little help from history in the form of the experience of other successful leaders. Study such examples not for the purpose of imitation, but to derive the principles that guided others to the results they wanted. Leave ample room for your own genius.

4

Tactics
and
Execution

Lesson 92
Why Flexibility Counts

> "When two armies are both on the defensive, the one that can most
> quickly concentrate several detachments to destroy an opposing
> force deployed in detachments manifestly would need fewer troops,
> and, with equal strength, would always win advantages."
>
> ~ "Notes on the Political and Military Position of Our Armies
> in Piedmont and Spain," June 1794

As with any organized body, no army is immune from the basic
principle of economics: *Resources are inherently scarce.* There are never
sufficient resources to satisfy every need and want. Management,
whether of a business or of an army, is therefore about the effective
allocation of resources.

In defensive warfare, in which both sides are essentially
defending a mutual frontier, Napoleon postulated that flexibility
of deployment—the ability to "quickly concentrate several detachments" wherever and whenever needed in order to "destroy an
opposing force deployed in detachments"—achieved two advantages. First, employing tactics of flexibility, you would need fewer
troops overall. Second, if your strength were, overall, equal to
that of the enemy, the ability to quickly concentrate troops
anywhere along a defensive line "would always win advantages"
by bringing superior numbers against the enemy force at a particular place and time.

Organizational nimbleness and agility—flexible and responsive
systems of communication, supervisory organization, work
group or team structures, and unambiguous spheres of authority

—can enable managers to concentrate resources where and when needed, thereby reducing the necessity of maintaining large and expensive resources that are often underused. Napoleon almost always led numerically inferior armies and therefore relied on intelligent strategy and tactics to enable him to concentrate troops where and when he needed them. His success dramatically demonstrates the advantages of what today's businesses call JIT (just in time) tactics, which can be applied to all business resources, from inventory to personnel.

■

Lesson 93
Own an Edge

"We do not march, we fly."

~ Major General Louis-Alexandre Berthier, on the
speed of Napoleon's Army of Italy, April 1796

Armies of the late eighteenth century moved at a stately pace. They were encumbered by supply wagons, heavy artillery, legions of camp followers, lack of discipline, and an abundance of red tape. These were all generally accepted as unalterable facts of military life. It was as if the officers of Europe's armies had gotten together and agreed on *slow* as the standard speed of war.

Napoleon's Army of Italy was at a grave disadvantage in terms of supply, weapons, and manpower. By the standard measures of military might, it was inferior to the armies of Austria and the other members of the First Coalition arrayed against it.

What could the Army of Italy possibly possess that would give it an edge over its enemies?

Napoleon seized on speed. It was the one thing the other armies, though bigger and better equipped, lacked. And so Napoleon decided that *his* army could and therefore would possess speed.

With it, he understood, he would be able to concentrate forces when and where they were needed, so that even if the enemy had a larger army, *he* could put more men in a particular place and at a particular time than the enemy had at that place at that time.

To achieve speed, Napoleon made a virtue of his army's shortages—there was less to carry, less to haul, less to drag the army down—and he drove his men at the sustained pace of a forced march. "We do not march, we fly," the future marshal Berthier commented. And it was to victory that Napoleon and his army flew.

Do not dwell on your deficiencies. Instead, identify what your competition lacks. Then focus on your actual and potential assets. Identify what you possess and what you can acquire. Develop these as your edge. Count on them to carry you to victory.

■

Lesson 94
Don't Just Play the Game, Change the Game

"We no longer understand anything; we are dealing with a young general who is sometimes in front of us, sometimes in our rear, sometimes in our flanks; one never knows how he is going to deploy himself. This kind of warfare is unbearable and violates all customary procedures."

~Hungarian officer captured at the Battle of Lodi (May 10, 1796), interrogated by Napoleon, whom the officer did not recognize

Napoleon and Napoleonic combat practices were game changers. That was their power. An outsider from Corsica and now a citizen of a nation whose bloody revolution had made it an outsider among the states of Europe, Napoleon did not set out to fight war better than everyone else; he sought to fight it differently. This left all of his opponents in the same state as the Hungarian officer: bewildered, bereft, and profoundly demoralized, incapable of following, let alone emulating, the paradigm shift Napoleon had carried off. They might as well have been trying to fight a new species of general.

In fact, Napoleon was not nearly as radical as his impact made him appear. As an assiduous student of the "Great Captains" of the past, he believed in certain unchanging rules of war, including speed, concentration of forces, and unity of command. The break with the rules as everyone else understood them came not in doctrine or strategy, but in execution.

Napoleon achieved far greater speed than any of his opponents, especially in his early campaigns in which his armies, of grim necessity, were small. (In later campaigns, most notoriously the catastrophic 1812 invasion of Russia, his massive forces were unwieldy, their numbers more liability than asset.) His ability to concentrate forces against the points where the usually larger enemy army happened to be spread thinnest relied on speed. He had to get his men where he wanted them before the enemy could reinforce weak positions. Even with inferior numbers, Napoleon and his army seemed to be everywhere. Using a combination of intensive reconnaissance, firsthand intelligence, and his own ability to put himself in the mind of the enemy general, he knew where to send his forces, which he had trained and equipped to get there fast. He typically held the enemy's front with a relatively small force while swinging his main force wide for a devastating flanking attack. Like a prizefighter who holds his opponent with a teasing right while bearing down on him with a massive left hook, Napoleon mastered the sucker punch.

Speed and the combat equivalent of razzle-dazzle were easy to plan but supremely difficult to execute. Through logistical genius and sheer force of will, Napoleon simultaneously kept his army united and coordinated, while maintaining sufficient flexibility to detach units as necessary to create diversions designed to facilitate a flanking attack. The result was that the enemy, accustomed to the stately pace of late eighteenth-century warfare, in which combat actions unfolded serially rather than simultaneously, could not cope with the multiple assaults coming at him. The game had changed, and Napoleon, having remade the rules, seemed to be the only player who knew them.

Business paradigms shift all the time. Competitors who fail either to initiate and lead or to overtake and lead find themselves confused, demoralized, and left behind. Game changers are seldom complex or even profound. Generally, they exploit a technological innovation or cultural shift.

Speed and thoroughness of execution are almost always the means by which the game is changed. Design your organization and your own working methods for speed, which means speed of thought as well as speed of execution. Recognize opportunity. Then think about it with the object of exploiting it immediately. Don't ease into it. Don't evolve out of it. Don't develop its potential. *Use* the opportunity before others do, and use it in ways others do not yet understand. It is execution, not thought, that your customers and your competitors see and feel.

Lesson 95
Check the Expiration Date

> "The plan which was adopted and which was good for the month
> of June counts for nothing at the end of September."
>
> ~Letter to the Directory, September 6, 1796

A prolific planner, Napoleon was downright prodigal in revising and discarding the plans he made. The great virtue of careful planning—that it brings stability to flux, order to chaos—is also the shortcoming of any plan. Time flows, and circumstances change. The plan of a year, a month, or a week ago may be wholly inadequate to conditions today.

Napoleon never abandoned the idea of careful planning, but he strove to build into each plan alternatives to anticipate likely developments and flexibility to allow for improvisation. Typically, every campaign plan included provisions for preserving a single line of operations along which the army could withdraw, if necessary, to a position from which a new plan could be instituted and executed. Alternatives, flexibility, and—not least of all—escape were the three indispensable components of a Napoleonic campaign plan. All were intended to transform a static document into a dynamic guide in a real world borne along by the rushing stream of time.

Cherish a plan above reality, and you have a plan for a world that no longer exists. All planning is time sensitive—or should be—and all plans must allow for their own modification. "Master plans" and "plans written in stone" soon go stale, stink, become unusable, and get dangerous.

■

Lesson 96

Know the Limits of Passive Obedience

> "[The instructions of a] minister or prince . . . are not military orders and do not require passive obedience."
>
> ~ "Observations on the Military Operations of the Campaigns of 1796 and 1797 in Italy," quoted in Jay Luvaas, *Napoleon on the Art of War*, 1999

The instructions of a minister or prince, Napoleon asserted, must be followed "both in spirit and conscience"; however, because they are not "military orders"—orders issued by a general in command at the battlefront—they "do not require passive obedience." On the contrary, they call for compliance based on the knowledge and judgment of those actually present at the front. Even a military order, Napoleon elaborated, demands "passive obedience" only if it is given by a superior officer "who knows the condition of affairs and can listen to the objections and provide explanations to those who must execute the order."

The power of any enterprise is the product of the active synergy of independent sets of eyes, ears, brains, and experience. To demand passive—absolute, blind, unquestioning—obedience from subordinates is to abandon 90 percent of the value of the human capital in your organization.

■

Lesson 97
Everything Depends on Execution

> "The art of war is a simple art and everything depends upon execution: there is nothing vague, everything is common sense, and nothing about it is ideological."
> ~From 1799, quoted in Jay Luvaas,
> *Napoleon on the Art of War*, 1999

While celebrated by history and his contemporaries alike as a master of global strategy, Napoleon, in writing about the "art of war," often put greater emphasis on execution than he did on doctrine or strategy. This was somewhat disingenuous, since Napoleon was a meticulous planner, but he did clearly believe that whereas the best strategy could be spoiled by inadequate execution, the poorest strategy could often be saved by adept execution. Such a triumph could not be scripted or planned. It had to be perceived, felt, and executed in real time during the course of actual battle. The ability to do this, Napoleon observed, "properly constitutes the genius for war."

Business begins and ends by engaging reality. Execute a brilliant plan poorly, and the real result will be failure, regardless of any theoretical outcome. Execute even a mediocre plan to take full advantage of an emerging situation, and the outcome may well be success beyond anything your strategy contemplated.

■

Lesson 98
Turn Liabilities into Assets

> "These companies . . . will be taken from among those men
> exempted from conscription because they are too short."
> ~Letter to General Louis-Alexandre Berthier, December 22, 1803

Ask someone to describe Napoleon, and you're guaranteed to get at least two items of "information":

1. He kept his hand tucked into his coat.

2. He was very short.

The first item is true, as far as it goes. But anyone who has looked at any number of historical portraits knows that every man who wanted to appear dignified stuck his hand in his coat. It was simply the thing to do.

The second item is false—and probably originated in a piece of British propaganda. Napoleon stood five-feet, six and a half inches at a time in which the low end of average height for a man was five-four. He was not tall for his times, but he was certainly not short.

We need to know this so we don't mistake his motive for creating a special "mounted" or "mobile" or "partisan" (he wasn't sure what to call it) company in every battalion of light infantry regiments. These special companies consisted of soldiers four-feet-eleven or shorter and officers no taller than five feet. They were armed with the lightest possible fusil muskets and rifled carbines and trained to follow the cavalry at a trot, "holding sometimes the boot of the rider and sometimes the mane of the horse," so that, at a moment's notice, they could mount briskly behind the rider for rapid transportation by the cavalry. These special companies were always to be maintained in readiness and on a war footing.

Napoleon's adversaries marveled at the speed with which he transferred troops from one place to another. Innovations like the "mobile companies" made such unprecedented speed possible.

Analyze your human assets and design your organization to make the optimum use of each member of the team. Napoleon understood that short stature, generally considered a liability in a soldier, could become an asset if the short man were matched with the right job—even if that job had to be newly invented. You cannot successfully leverage your human assets if you insist on a single standard and an inflexible approach in which one size is forced to "fit" all.

■

Lesson 99
Take Good Care of the Soldier

> "Take good care of the soldier and look after him in detail."
>
> ~ Letter to General Auguste-Frédéric-Louis Marmont,
> March 12, 1804

No historical figure had a greater impact on the destiny of nations than Napoleon, yet his most radical policy was directed not at entire populations but at the individual soldier.

He instructed one of his generals, Auguste-Frédéric-Louis Marmont, to make it a practice, every time he arrived at camp, to assemble his troops facing each other by battalion and to inspect them, "one by one, for the next eight hours." Napoleon specifically directed the general to "listen to their complaints" and also to inspect their arms and "satisfy yourself that they do not lack anything."

Inspection by superior officers was certainly not new in Napoleon's time, but the notion of a general officer inspecting troops in detail—and for an entire day!—was radical. Even more outlandish was the idea that the *general* should listen to the *complaints* of the private soldier. In the armies of Napoleon's day, the soldier's lot truly was "not to reason why, but to do and die."

World War I, fought little more than a hundred years after the Napoleonic Wars, introduced the concept of the Unknown Soldier, the unidentified casualty whose burial with honors was intended to represent all the slain troops who could not be identified. The presumption by the time of World War I was that the "unknowns" were a minority, that the army made it a practice to identify and individually bury and honor all those who had given their lives. We take this concept for granted today, but in the early nineteenth century, as in all previous history, common soldiers were by policy and definition unknowns. No effort was made to identify them. They were anonymous in life and death, almost always consigned to a common grave, typically on the field where they fell. Napoleon did not end this practice, but he did insist on treating each *living* soldier as a valued human being rendering valued service to his country. He believed that this was essential to victory, and he would surely have seconded what one of his latter-day admirers, General George S. Patton Jr., said over a century after Napoleon's death: "The soldier is the army."

> ***The soldier is the army.*** The organization you lead is not you. It is not the state-of-the-art equipment it may own. And it is not the legal papers that incorporated it. The organization is not even your management team, your best salesperson, your most imaginative creative director.
>
> The organization you lead is the entry-level hire who is paid the lowest wage. "Look after him in detail."

■

Lesson 100
Always Enough

> "One always has enough troops when he knows how to use them
> and when generals do not sleep in the towns but instead bivouac
> with their troops."
>
> ~Letter to Joseph Bonaparte, June 26, 1806

Sufficiency of resources, as Napoleon saw it, was not a matter of any set quantity, but of knowing how to use what one had. For an incompetent commander, no army was large enough, whereas a skilled general could work wonders with the smallest of forces.

Knowing how to effectively use the troops one has, Napoleon believed, came from training and inborn military genius combined with intimate knowledge of the troops and a willingness to share their fate. A general who held himself aloof from his command could never hope to use his soldiers adequately, whatever their number.

Effective leadership is largely about using resources with maximum efficiency. The skill required to achieve this is best acquired by firsthand experience with every phase of an organization's work, and it is most effectively applied firsthand as well, by a manager who leads from the shop floor, not the executive penthouse.

■

Lesson 101
The Uncertainty Principle

"Keep in mind that nothing is more uncertain than the art of firing."

~Letter to Joseph Bonaparte, June 26, 1806

For all his reliance on mathematics in war and his consequent eleva-tion of artillery above all other service branches, Napoleon confessed to his brother Joseph that nothing was "more uncertain than the art of firing" artillery. Although firing was "classified among the physio-mathematical sciences," Napoleon wrote, "yet its results are dubious."

But if the results of science were "dubious," the results "of prac-tice are certain." Based in mathematical *theory*, the *practice* of artillery depended, according to Napoleon, on practice. That is what makes its science work in the real world.

> **Soak up all** you can of management and leadership theory, but be aware that only practice will fill the gaps of uncertainty when it comes to drawing a bead on high-stakes decisions.

■

Lesson 102
Take Pleasure in Reading Your Muster Rolls

"I get more pleasure from this kind of reading than a young girl gets from reading a novel."

~Letter to Joseph Bonaparte, August 20, 1806

For most of us, nothing could make for drier reading than an inven-tory—and a "muster roll," a register of officers and men in military units, is first and last an inventory. To Napoleon, the committed general, nothing was more pleasurable than doing what he advised his brother Joseph to do: spend an hour every morning reading the muster rolls of his armies.

It was not merely the perverse pleasure a wonk takes in technical details. The "muster rolls" of any organization reveal who does what and who is where. It is a way of knowing the exact position and composition of each unit in your army. The pleasure of such knowledge is empowerment. For Napoleon, platoons, companies, regiments, and armies were not marks on a map, but human teams of leaders and followers, planners and executors. He made it his business to know the special strengths and weaknesses of each. And he always kept this knowledge up to the minute. In this way, he leveraged his resources and minimized waste of personnel, equipment, and time.

> **Know your enterprise** as individuals and team members. Know what they can do and what they cannot do. Know where they are and where they are not. Refresh this knowledge constantly. Take pleasure in this task as you would take pleasure in any productive and empowering activity.

■

Lesson 103
Common Sense Cuts Red Tape

> "[In war, grant] as much as possible without any formality except
> for the returns that help keep things accurate."
> ~Letter to Minister of War Jean-François-Aimé Dejean,
> March 25, 1807

In war, Napoleon observed, "delay is fatal." Common sense therefore dictates minimizing delay, which means cutting red tape whenever and wherever it is found.

In a letter to his minister of war, Napoleon presented a hypothetical situation in which a cavalry regiment was found to have 300 dismounted men in its depot with only twelve or fifteen horses between them. "One has to make inquires [as to the disparity between horses and men,]" Napoleon wrote, "but start first off by giving [the regiment] 300 horses, 300 saddles, and 300 bridles, so that this regiment provides me with 300 effectives in the presence of the enemy." A single dismounted soldier in a cavalry depot is not only a waste, but, in time of battle, dangerous. "There is always time later to put things in order." In exchange for the "false sense of economy" red tape formalities provide, you may well have to sacrifice victory.

Companies are often rigidly divided into "front-office" and "back-office" functions, revenue generators and those who account for and otherwise manage revenue in and revenue out. In too many organizations, the back office gets in the way of the front office or is perceived to do so: "red tape" slows production, interferes with sales, takes too much time. The purpose of a business is to make money, not record the transfer of money.

Common sense dictates that nothing should interfere with the core of any business, which is creating value, and such functions as accounting and tracking should never even appear to take precedence over what is being accounted for or tracked. That is common sense.

Uncommon sense dictates working to eliminate the outworn distinction between front and back office. Every part of the office should be dedicated to creating value, seamlessly. Accounting and tracking functions should not merely follow, but lead, speed, and facilitate revenue-generating activities. At best, they should be predictive of needs. At the very least, they should operate simultaneously with those needs. If Napoleon's war minister had been doing his job correctly, every cavalryman would have had a horse, saddle, and bridle, and there would be no deficiency to correct.

Lesson 104
The Real Cost of Wasted Effort

"We must not exhaust the troops in needless marches and coun-
termarches. We must not assume that when we have made one
false march of three or four days that we could make up for it by
one countermarch: this is usually committing two mistakes
instead of one."

> ~ "Notes on the Actual Position of the Army in Spain,
> July 21, 1808," quoted in Jay Luvaas,
> *Napoleon on the Art of War*, 1999

Common sense would dictate that a wasted march–a mistaken
movement in one direction–must be corrected by a *countermarch*–a
march in the opposite direction. Thus a wasted effort has an initial
cost, *a*, which must be corrected by another expenditure, *b*, making
the total cost of the error $a + b$. That is bad enough. But Napoleon
asserted that taking the commonsense measure of correcting a
march with a countermarch does not simply add two expenditures
of time and effort, but also fails to correct the original error. Indeed,
it creates a new one.

In any complex, high-stakes endeavor, whether in war or in
business, the misplaced investment of resources can rarely be
"undone" by simple reallocation. Mistakenly stepping into a
situation typically creates conditions that cannot be corrected
simply by backing out of the situation. Wasted effort may not
create the results you want, but it almost always creates results,
which must then be figured into plans moving forward. Engage
the situation as it presents itself, not as you wanted it to be
before you marched in the wrong direction. Fail to do this, and
you will only compound the initial error.

■

Lesson 105
Specify, Specify, Specify

> "Give the length, width, and quality . . . rivers . . . traced and mea-
> sured . . . bridges and fords marked . . . number of houses and inhab-
> itants . . . indicated . . . measure the heights of hills and mountains."
> ~Letter to General Henri-Jacques-Guillaume Clarke,
> December 19, 1809

"When I ask for a reconnaissance," Napoleon wrote, "I do not want . . . a plan of campaign." To ensure that he got nothing of the kind, Napoleon even banned engineers from using the very word *enemy*. All he wanted from them was a thorough and detailed account of roads, including their condition, slopes, heights, gorges, and obstacles. He wanted to know where vehicles could travel and where they could not. Instead of the language of war, strategy, struggle, or tactics, he wanted the specific language of mapping. Everything was to be drawn carefully and accurately, with the scale of all maps consistent. He wanted measurements of everything–road length and width, the width and depth of rivers, the dimensions of fording places, the number of houses and inhabitants in villages along the route of march, the elevation of hills and mountains, and the conditions–so far as the feasibility of movement was concerned–of everything.

It was not the language of glory, politics, strategy, or combat that Napoleon wanted, but of logistics. It is a language not of inspiration, courage, and patriotism, but of numbers and the objective evaluation of physical facts. In its place, an eloquent call to battle is indispensable to victory. In *its* place the specificity of measurement is equally indispensable.

Leaders of any business enterprise must be fluent in many languages. They must speak the languages of vision, inspiration, motivation, correction, warning, and reprimand. Above all, however, they must speak the language of business, which is the expression of everything in quantifiable specifics, especially money spent, money saved, money made, and money lost. CEOs and managers must always know when to speak *this* language and only this language, avoiding, for the time being at least, any other.

■

Lesson 106
Test Belief against Outcome

"We believed . . . but experience has shown."
~Letter to General Auguste-Frédéric-Louis Marmont,
October 13, 1813

The Napoleonic Wars were fought during a time of transition for the infantry, and Napoleon was instrumental in that transition. During eighteenth-century combat, muskets were fired in simultaneous volleys by ranks of soldiers. Because the muskets of the era had to be loaded through the muzzle in a laborious and time-consuming process, techniques were developed to increase the rate of fire. Soldiers in the French and Indian War (1754–63) and the American Revolution (1775–83) were arrayed in three ranks to deliver volleys of fire. The front, or first, rank would fire, then retire behind the third rank to reload, putting the second rank in front, which would fire, retire behind the original first rank to reload, putting the third rank in front, and so on. By the era of the Napoleonic Wars at the start of the nineteenth century, three ranks of shooters were still employed in the French army, but the drill had changed somewhat. The first rank would fire from a kneeling position, so that the second rank, behind them, could fire over them, and the soldiers of the third rank would rest the barrels of their muskets on the right shoulder of the second-rank shooters, so that they could fire simultaneously. Thus all three ranks delivered a simultaneous volley.

Often, the ranks would divide themselves into left and right platoons. While the left platoon fired, the right would reload. While it fired, the left reloaded, and so on.

Napoleon and others examined this firing drill, which combined the time-honored three ranks with an innovation to promote more rapid fire. He concluded that, in actual combat, firing at will, rather than in simultaneous mechanical volleys, had become more effective. He also concluded that having the third rank fire over the shoulder of the second rank was hazardous to the second as well as first ranks. It was decided to reduce the firing ranks and to assign the third rank to the task of reloading the weapons of the front two. Napoleon and others "believed" that this would increase the volume of fire, but "experience" soon showed that the second rank fired no more rapidly using this method than it did before, and, furthermore, it fired less accurately. Napoleon therefore decided to do away with the three-rank firing formation altogether.

At first, he (and others) experimented with two ranks, but Napoleon ultimately concluded that the "fire of skirmishers—that is, accurate firing at will against specific targets—is best of all," with the volley fire of a single rank second best, and that of two ranks "still good." He accordingly changed the way large infantry formations fired their shoulder weapons.

Conventional commanders were reluctant to abandon the three-rank formation, but when experience contradicted belief and assumption, Napoleon did not hesitate to follow experience.

If you would grow your business, and make it more competitive, more efficient, and more profitable, accept the leadership principle that *experience trumps belief*. Confronted with the results of experience, discard belief as you would any other consumable your business uses and throws away.

■

Lesson 107
Demand Efficiency

"You will see the advantage this offers."
~Letter to General Auguste-Frédéric-Louis Marmont,
October 13, 1813

Napoleon became forceful in his insistence on reducing the three-rank firing formation to two. He had concluded that the third rank was "of no use in firing and less so for the bayonet." The two-rank formation, he explained, would not only *reduce* a waste of manpower, it would actually *increase* the efficiency of the force by one-third. Moreover, because they were accustomed to seeing the French army arrayed three deep and the two-rank formation would spread the army out, the enemy commanders would overestimate the French strength by another third. Thus the two-rank formation would actually leverage available numbers not by one-third but by two-thirds.

The marvel of most of Napoleon's campaigns was that he prevailed against superior numbers. He always found ways to increase the efficiency of his forces—through superior training, superior tactics, and the careful crafting of an illusion of greater numbers than he actually possessed. Whereas conventional commanders continually demanded larger and larger armies, Napoleon questioned accepted practices to leverage the resources he had available. Mere numbers were less effective against an enemy than ensuring that he attained the highest possible performance from the resources he possessed.

To write off Napoleon as "power mad" is to discard the most useful lessons to be learned from his approach to success in combat. As a leader of armies, his primary objective was not so much to amass larger forces but to devise practices that would multiply the effectiveness of the forces available. His obsession was less with power than with the optimal leveraging of power. The "holy grail" he sought was efficiency.

Lesson 108
Force an Attack

> "If the enemy occupies a strong position you must occupy a position that will force him to attack you."
>
> ~ Quoted in Jay Luvaas, *Napoleon on the Art of War*, 1999

Aggressive generals are usually successful generals. Wars are seldom won by defense. But Napoleon recognized that, under certain circumstances, the greatest advantage comes neither in attacking nor in defending but instead in compelling an enemy to attack from a position favorable to you and unfavorable to him. This was, Napoleon concluded, the best approach to engaging an enemy who occupies a strong position. The problem, of course, is how to draw the enemy out of that favorable position. Napoleon did this by occupying a position that forced the enemy to emerge and attack him. Then, Napoleon would wage an active defense from his own favorable position against an attacker who had given up the advantage of position in order to attack.

"For where your treasure is, there will your heart be also," wrote Luke in his gospel. He might have been describing a favorite Napoleonic tactic, which can be applied against any strong adversary or competitor. To draw an adversary into the open, to compel him to leave the place of his greatest strength and security, you must threaten something he values.

As an invading army may draw defenders out of their fortresses by threatening their capital city, you may coax a competitor to relinquish the advantages of the status quo by threatening something important to him. You are a customer service manager. John is a sales manager. You know that the leadership of your firm has traditionally favored sales over customer service. A larger departmental management position opens up. You go for it, knowing that doing so will likely prompt John to go for it as well—even though he feels secure in his sales role. Most likely, John will beat you in the competition, but, even if he does, you will have "forced" him out of his tightly held sales niche, which you can then move into. Of course, if corporate leadership surprises you and promotes you instead of John, that is even better—but achieving the lesser goal of moving into sales management (valued more highly by your company) is still a big victory.

■

Lesson 109

Hide Weakness while Building Strength

"When the conquest of a country is undertaken by two or three armies, which have each their separate line of operation, until they arrive at a point fixed upon for their concentration, it should be laid down as a principle, that the union of these different corps should never take place near the enemy: because the enemy, in uniting his forces, may not only prevent this junction, but may beat the armies in detail."

~Military Maxim IV

Until its disparate elements are united, the strongest army can be defeated piecemeal or, as military professionals express it, can be "defeated in detail." Therefore (Napoleon believed), the union of dispersed forces should take place before the enemy is reached and never in the presence (or "face") of the enemy.

Display a united front. Argument is essential to the creative process, but it should be hidden from those outside the group. If your work group or management team is not yet united on an issue or course of action, make no presentations internally, within your organization, or externally, to clients and others, until you have reached consensus. Unity is perceived as strength, disunity as weakness.

Lesson 110
Test Yourself

> "A general-in-chief should ask himself frequently in the day, 'What
> should I do if the enemy's army appeared now in my front, or on
> my right, or my left?' If he has any difficulty in answering these
> questions, his position is bad, and he should seek to remedy it."
>
> ~ Military Maxim VIII

One side's complacency is the other side's ally. Napoleon kept complacency at bay not through destructive self-doubt, but through
healthy self-questioning. If he could not answer his own tactical
question to his satisfaction, he set about creating the conditions that
would allow him to make a satisfactory answer. Thus, if he found
himself unable to say what he would do if the enemy suddenly
appeared "in my front, or on my right, or my left," he knew that he
had to reposition the army to allow for a satisfactory answer.

Do not passively trust to the adequacy of your assumptions.
Continually test them. Based on the results of this testing, take
steps to bring assumptions and reality into perfect alignment.
No manager can afford complacency.

Lesson 111

The Morale of Momentum Is the Momentum of Morale

> "The strength of an army, like the power in mechanics, is esti-
> mated by multiplying the mass by the rapidity; a rapid march aug-
> ments the morale of an army, and increases its means of victory.
> Press on!"
>
> ~Military Maxim IX

Napoleon was outnumbered throughout most of his military career,
yet, more often than not, the outnumbered Napoleon was victorious. He understood what his adversaries often failed to understand: Numbers are but one term in the equation of battle. Rapidity
of movement is the other. Multiply a relatively small number by a
high degree of rapidity, and the product is superior to that of the
enemy. Not only does speed allow a force to reach an advantageous
position before the enemy can, it also "augments the morale of an
army" because the intelligent use of energy is always invigorating
and encouraging.

Operating in a large organization can be a source of pride,
confidence, and optimism, or it can be an alienating and dis-
heartening experience. Creating an environment of decisive,
rapid action is always important to efficient execution and
morale, but its importance increases in proportion to the size
of the organization. Big organizations continually need to
prove, both to others and to themselves, that they are not
bogged down by bureaucracy or mired in the status quo, but
can move nimbly, quickly, decisively, and effectively.

■

Lesson 112
Obey the Laws of Compensation

> "When an army is inferior in number, inferior in cavalry, and in artillery, it is essential to avoid a general action. The first deficiency should be supplied by rapidity of movement; the want of artillery, by the nature of the maneuvers; and the inferiority in cavalry, by the choice of positions. In such circumstances the morale of the soldier does much."
>
> ~ Military Maxim X

Napoleon assiduously avoided operating from assumptions based on best-case scenarios. This did not mean, however, that he retreated into pessimism. Instead, whenever he recognized a deficiency, he looked for ways to compensate. Inferiority in numbers could be compensated for by rapidity of movement. The enemy's superior numbers meant nothing if you could position your forces to oppose his weakest point before he is able reinforce it. A shortage of artillery could be compensated for by maneuvers to bring more of the artillery you do have into effective action, and a deficiency of cavalry could be compensated for by taking up a position that forces the enemy into terrain that makes the use of cavalry difficult or impossible. Finally, superiority of morale blunts the adverse effect of all varieties of deficiency.

Play to your strengths, not to your weaknesses. Rather than dwell on deficiency, develop strengths. Use what you have to compensate for what you lack.

Lesson 113
Go Ahead, Put All Your Eggs in One Basket

"An army ought to have only one line of operation. This should be preserved with care, and never abandoned but in the last extremity."

~ Military Maxim XII

The line of operation, through which an army travels to attain its objective, must be kept open to the rear, so that there is a continuous avenue of communications, reinforcement, and resupply as well as a route for withdrawal and retreat, if need be. Whereas many commanders seek to open up multiple lines of operation, arguing that it is better to have more than one avenue of communications, supply, reinforcement, and escape, Napoleon consistently stressed the importance of maintaining just one. He argued that a single line was an asset readily defended, whereas multiple lines put a burden on defense, forcing a general to take men from his offensive forces. Instead of multiplying safety, according to Napoleon, multiple lines of operations multiplied vulnerability by creating more targets for enemy attack.

> **The principle of** redundancy in "mission-critical" applications is so ingrained that most managers invest in a multiplicity of systems without giving much thought to their return on investment. Make it a practice to question redundancy before accepting or, for that matter, rejecting it. Anything that fails to create demonstrable value must be regarded as a liability rather than an asset.

■

Lesson 114
Demand Control

> "It is an approved maxim in war, never to do what the enemy wishes
> you to do, for this reason alone, that he desires it. A field of battle, there-
> fore, which he has previously studied and reconnoitered, should be
> avoided, and double care should be taken where he has had time to
> fortify and entrench. One consequence deducible from this principle is,
> never to attack a position in front which you can gain by turning."
>
> ~Military Maxim XVI

We may accuse a person who demands control of absolutely everything—even minutiae that seem of little consequence—of harboring
a "Napoleonic complex." Such a diagnosis is intended as a criticism,
of course, but Napoleon himself would find the accusation a cause
for congratulation. His policy and his practice were to demand or
seize control of everything. If he needed a reason for *assuming* control, he looked no further than the fact that his adversary did not
want to *relinquish* control.

A general's first duty was to deny the enemy anything and
everything, beginning with the choice of battlefield. As Napoleon
saw it, this did not necessarily mean avoiding battle where one
happened to encounter the enemy, but it did call for attacking to
force the enemy to turn from the front he had defensively prepared.
Napoleon freely favored flanking attacks and almost always
eschewed frontal attacks. He believed it irrational to expect to win a
battle that began with giving up control of important choices.

History offers many examples in which victory is snatched
from the proverbial jaws of defeat; however, history offers far
more examples of battles that both began and ended successfully. Victory usually both begins and ends with winning moves.
Never embark on a project by surrendering any aspect of control. Endeavor to begin in triumph.

Lesson 115

Always Manage Recovery

> "When an army is driven from a first position, the retreating columns
> should rally always sufficiently in the rear, to prevent any interruption
> from the enemy. The greatest disaster that can happen is when the
> columns are attacked in detail, and before their junction."
>
> ~Military Maxim XXVII

Retreat is both physically dangerous—an army fights from its front, not its rear—and psychologically demoralizing. Napoleon had repeatedly seen the effects of such demoralization in any number of enemies he defeated. An army in retreat tends to stop being an army. It does not become a mob, but a mere collection of individuals who think and act only for themselves.

In retreat, the natural impulse is to get away. Rallying and regrouping are not spontaneous acts for an army in defeat. These actions must be instigated, imposed, and led by the general in charge. But while rallying and regrouping are absolutely necessary to prevent a rout, the seasoned general will resist his own impulse to re-form his army prematurely. Instead, as Napoleon advised, he will rally the retreating columns "always sufficiently in the rear, to prevent any interruption from the enemy." Armies are easy to defeat when their constituents are fragmented, but much harder to defeat when their parts are fully coalesced and coordinated. In leading a retreat, a skilled general gives himself sufficient distance from the enemy to ensure that the fragments of his army are reunited before he re-engages.

Reverses naturally create panic, disorder, and demoralization. Teams fragment, their members no longer thinking and acting with regard to the group, but in fear and anxiety for their own individual welfare. Converting disaster into recovery requires fearless management. Start by giving yourself and your team the space it needs to rally. Don't rush a recovery. Plan and manage it as you would any other operation or initiative.

Lesson 116
Prepare for Maximum Effort

> "No force should be detached on the eve of a battle, because affairs may change during the night, either by the retreat of the enemy, or by the arrival of large reinforcements to enable him to resume the offensive, and counteract your previous arrangements."
>
> ~ Military Maxim XXVIII

> "When you have resolved to fight a battle, collect your whole force. Dispense with nothing. A single battalion sometimes decides the day."
>
> ~ Military Maxim XXIX

Napoleon's aim was always to commit everything available to every battle. If he judged a battle worth fighting, it was worth the maximum effort.

There is no such thing as a half-hearted commitment. If an endeavor is worth undertaking, it must be worth committing to with all available resources. Doubts sufficiently compelling to prevent commitment are ample reason to rethink, modify, postpone, or scrap any initiative.

■

Lesson 117
Apply Thought to Everything

> "Encampments of the same army should always be formed so as to protect each other."
>
> ~ Military Maxim XXXV

No element of Napoleon's ideal army was ever permitted to be idle or inert. Between battles, when military formations were encamped and to all appearances completely inactive, one camp nevertheless continued to function to protect another. Achieving this level of productive activity even in rest required the artful deployment of each encampment.

> **Apply thought to** every element of your organization. Untapped resources are liabilities. Only when a resource is made to produce does it become an asset. Think of ways to make every resource productive all the time. This is dynamic management.

■

Lesson 118
Think the Unthinkable

> "A fortified place can only protect the garrison and detain the enemy for a certain time. When this time has elapsed, and the defenses of the place are destroyed, the garrison should lay down its arms. All civilized nations are agreed on this point. . . . At the same time, there are generals . . . who are of opinion that a governor should never surrender, but . . . should blow up the fortifications, and take advantage of the night to cut . . . through the besieging army. . . . [Such generals] have often brought off three-fourths of their garrison."
>
> ~Military Maxim XLV

Napoleon was no fanatic. He acknowledged that there was a time to cut your losses by surrender. For a garrison to hold a fortress to the last man was suicidal and therefore served no purpose. "All civilized nations are agreed on this point," he wrote.

And yet he acknowledged generals who believe that the "governor" of a fortress should never surrender, "but that in the last extremity he should blow up the fortifications, and take advantage of the night to cut his way through the besieging army." To those who would label as unthinkable this departure from the course of conduct accepted by "civilized nations," Napoleon here extended an invitation to *think about it*: in a dire situation, saving three-fourths of your resources is hardly a suicidal outcome of combat.

> **Received wisdom**—the collections of principles and precepts so widely accepted as to seem self-evident—is a valuable body of knowledge to study and to know, but it is wholly without value as a replacement for thought and judgment carried out in the experience of events in real time. Nothing should be deemed so out of bounds as to be unthinkable.

Lesson 119
Leadership by Detail

> "Tents are unfavorable to health. The soldier is best when he bivouacs, because he sleeps with his feet to the fire, which speedily dries the ground on which he lies. A few planks, or a little straw, shelter him from the wind.
>
> "On the other hand, tents are necessary for the superior officers, who have to write and to consult their maps. . . . Tents are always objects of observation to the enemy's staff. They afford information in regard to your numbers and the ground you occupy."
> ~Military Maxim LXII

No general thought in larger terms than Napoleon and yet perhaps none habitually drilled down so deeply into the layers of command detail. Napoleon never forgot that, in the end, an army is not a mass of men, but men—each one an individual—and he was always concerned for their welfare, because he understood that the welfare of each man was the welfare of the entire army.

He had sound, detailed reasons for rejecting tents to shelter enlisted men while embracing their use for officers. The distinction he drew had nothing to do with military rank or social class and everything to do with function. An enlisted soldier needed his feet to the fire, whereas an officer needed a place to read maps and to write. Moreover, the restriction of tents to officers' use served a tactical function, making it more difficult for an enemy to accurately estimate the size of one's force.

In modern leadership circles, *micromanagement* is a dirty word, but the great leaders, in all times and places, never hesitate to seize on the important details and take a hands-on approach to command. Leadership at the top is not about "rising above" the details. It is about understanding and managing the links between the key details and the big picture, ensuring that there is no disconnect between the two. It is about knowing which details most directly affect overall and final outcomes and ensuring that these are not ignored but managed effectively.

■

Lesson 120
Exploit the Marginal Advantage

"There is a moment in every battle at which the least manoeuvre is decisive and gives superiority, as one drop of water causes overflow."

~Napoleon at St. Helena, quoted in
Felix Markham, *Napoleon*, 1963

Years of combat experience taught Napoleon that most battles were quite evenly matched, with casualties on both sides very nearly equal. The difference between defeat and victory was typically a very thin margin. This being the case, the outcome of the battle was almost always decided by some minor maneuver or advantage gained, not some overwhelming breakthrough. Victory came not in a torrent, but in much the same way that a single "drop of water causes overflow." This being the case, Napoleon squandered no advantage, no matter how slight, and he stood ready to exploit every marginal advantage, recognizing that each might bring victory.

Victory need not be triumphant, nor defeat catastrophic. Most competitions in business are decided by a few percentage points or a few dollars, especially in established firms and mature markets. Wins in business are usually marginal, and this means that no advantage or loss of ground, no matter how apparently slight, can be ignored. The thick of the competitive struggle, whether between businesses or between co-workers in the same firm, is at the margins. Don't expect to make a killing, but do aim to edge out the competition by the paper-thin space of a few fractions. Dimes make dollars, and dollars make profits.

■

5

Motivation
and
Communication

Lesson 121
Give Them a Name

> "An ordinary officer would never have questioned the traditional numerical designation [of artillery batteries]. Napoleon changed numbers to names."
>
> ~Robert Asprey, *The Rise of Napoleon Bonaparte*, 2000

In the summer of 1793, the city of Marseille rose up against the Convention that was creating the revolutionary government of France. Soon, under Royalist influence, the city of Toulon teetered on the verge of following Marseille's lead. Moreover, the English fleet, cruising offshore, was ready to pounce in support of any counter-revolutionary insurrection. Napoleon, at the time a young captain of artillery, took charge of the batteries at Toulon and put them into position to drive the English ships away.

The artillery batteries bore nothing but the numerical designations given them when the army belonged to Louis XVI. Although he was a junior officer, whose authority extended only to commanding the batteries, Napoleon saw fit to replace their numerical designations with names that gave them a revolutionary identity. Acting unilaterally, he christened his units "the Battery of the Montagnards," "the Battery of the Sans Culottes," "the Battery of the Jacobins," "the Battery of the Men without Fear," and so on.

Napoleon wanted his men to think of themselves as soldiers upholding the Revolution, not as ciphers in units distinguished by nothing more than their emotionally neutral and therefore ultimately meaningless numbers. He surely exceeded his authority by naming the batteries, but in consideration of the role they played in saving the Revolution, no one dared step in to restore the old system of numbers.

A team is only as good as its name. Do everything in your power to create a distinctive and proud identity for the members of your enterprise, an identity that connects them to something greater than themselves and that therefore makes each of them more powerful.

■

Lesson 122
Man Your Post

"I have always found Napoleon at his post; if he needed rest he slept on the ground wrapped in his cloak, he never left his batteries."
~ General François Amédée Doppet reporting on Artillery Captain Napoleon Bonaparte at the 1793 Battle of Toulon, quoted in Robert Asprey, *The Rise of Napoleon Bonaparte*, 2000

From the beginning of his career, Napoleon earned a reputation for always being everywhere he needed to be. He believed his personal presence at the front was essential to victory. When he departed from this policy during the Peninsular War in Spain and Portugal (1807–1814) by delegating battle to his marshals and generals, the result was a defeat that contributed to his abdication and the dissolution of the empire he had built.

Be available. Email, videoconferencing, instant messaging, remote computing, and such tools as a corporate intranet allow you to be in touch at all times no matter where you are and without having to wrap yourself in your cloak to snatch a few minutes' sleep on the cold, hard ground.
   Your presence—digitally or in person—is essential to victory.

■

Lesson 123
Redefine Confidence

> "The administrative situation is dreadful, but not hopeless."
>
> ~Letter to the Directory, March 28, 1796

In 1792, during the late phase of the French Revolution, several European powers created what history calls the First Coalition in an effort first to contain and then to destroy the upstart French Republic. The struggle seesawed between the outnumbered French forces and those of the Coalition until June 29, 1795, when an Austrian army attacked the French Army of Italy, which had been reduced by disease and other causes to an effective force of no more than 37,000. The Directory dispatched to the Italian front the commander who had saved the Revolution against the Royalist uprising of 13 Vendémiarie (October 5, 1795), Napoleon Bonaparte, appointing him commander-in-chief of the Army of Italy on March 2, 1796.

Doubtless, many, jealous and fearful of Napoleon's meteoric rise, hoped he would fail in what was a desperate assignment to command the puniest and most woefully neglected of the French Republic's thirteen field armies. If Napoleon was appalled by the condition of his forces, he did not let on. Although his poorly trained, poorly equipped, hungry, and demoralized 37,000 faced more than 50,000 Austrians at the time of his arrival on the front on March 27, he reported to the Directory the following day that the situation, while "dreadful," was not "hopeless."

In essence, he redefined confidence. For him, *confidence* was no longer a belief in success, but a belief in the *hope* of success. It was now his job to transform *hope* into accomplished *fact*.

Napoleon began that transformation by presenting hope to his soldiers as something tangible, solid, and golden. "Soldiers," he addressed them, "you are ill-clothed, poorly fed; the government owes you much, it has given you nothing."

Hearing this, Napoleon's soldiers knew that he understood them.

Napoleon continued: "I will lead you to the richest plains in the world. Rich provinces and great cities will be in your power; you will find there honor, glory, and riches." What made this promised transformation believable was the change from the collective, impersonal noun—"the government"—to singular, personal pronouns: *I* and *you*: "*I* will lead *you*." The soldiers, left hopeless by *the government*, were hungry for the hope this *I* promised. Desperate to believe, ready to believe, they believed.

Within two weeks, on April 12, the new commander launched a daring attack at Montenotte in northwestern Italy, defeating the stunned Austrians. He followed this with another victory at the Battle of Dego on April 14–15. Napoleon knew that the ragtag army would be invigorated by these triumphs—practically reborn—and he next led it in a full-scale invasion of Piedmont, which culminated on April 28 in the Armistice of Cherasco between France and Piedmont.

In just three weeks, Napoleon victoriously concluded a war that had raged for more than three years. His success brought massive reinforcements to the Army of Italy, which Napoleon used to bring about a triumphant end to the War of the First Coalition when he dictated the terms of the Treaty of Campo Formio on October 17, 1797, by which Belgium was ceded to France, and French control of the Rhineland and much of Italy was recognized. The eleven-hundred-year-old Republic of Venice was divided up between Austria and France.

Far from having been extinguished by the First Coalition, the French Republic, thanks to Napoleon, was on its way to empire.

In a crisis, the only attitude more dangerous than empty optimism is hopelessness. Acknowledge and understand all difficulties, deficiencies, obstacles, and threats, then recalibrate your confidence accordingly. Base it on rational hope and make plans to transform hope into accomplished fact.

■

Lesson 124
Bestow an Identity

> "[You will] be able to say with pride: 'I serve with the army that conquered Italy.'"
>
> ~ Address to troops, April 26, 1796

Napoleon was renowned for the stirring speeches he made to his soldiers. Those in search of the magic that created an empire have pored over his speeches, hoping to crack the code. But the magic of inspiration is not in some secret Napoleonic eloquence. Its source is both less complex and more difficult. Napoleon knew how to reflect to his army its own achievements.

He transformed himself into a mirror, which he held up to his army. He had the ability to show them their own best selves, and he set this as the mark they were to make over and over again. The greatest gift he gave his army was not his tactical genius, but the gift of their own identity as soldiers who could achieve miracles:

> Soldiers! In fifteen days you have won six victories, taken twenty-one standards, fifty-five cannon, several fortresses, you have conquered the richest part of the Piedmont; you have taken fifteen thousand prisoners, killed or wounded more than ten thousand men . . . deprived of everything, you have made up for everything. You have won battles without cannon, crossed rivers without bridges, made forced marches without shoes, bivouacked without brandy and without bread.

Having reflected these miracles back upon his army, Napoleon asked them for more by holding up a different mirror, one that revealed to the men their identity *brought forward* into the future:

> The greatest obstacles are without doubt surmounted; but you still have battles ahead, cities to take, rivers to cross. Is the courage of any of you weakening? Would any of you prefer to return to the mountains and suffer the abuses of

military slavery? No . . . [e]very single one of you wants to extend the glory of the French race; to humiliate those arrogant kings who dare think of putting us in irons; to dictate a glorious peace which will indemnify the country for its immense sacrifices; everybody wants, upon returning to their villages, to be able to say with pride: "I serve with the army that conquered Italy."

The great leaders are those who bestow an identity upon their enterprise, an identity that empowers everyone in the organization to imagine their best selves, selves triumphant, selves capable of achievements they had never before imagined on their own. This is the heart and soul of inspirational motivation. This is the foundation on which excellence is built.

■

Lesson 125
Speak the Language of Business

> "You can now count on 6 to 8 million gold or silver ingots or jewels, which are at your disposal in Genoa."
> ~Report to the Directory, May 22, 1796

To win continued support for his ambitious military campaign in Italy, Napoleon wrote not of the prodigies of glory he was achieving, but of the money he was making for France. In his report, he took care both to quantify the haul he had made and to break it down into its major and eminently fungible constituents: gold, silver, and jewels.

Both Napoleon and the Directory spoke French, of course, but
Napoleon understood that the perpetually cash-strapped revolutionary government found another language far more persuasive. It was the language of business, which is the language
of money: money out and money in, money lost and money
made. When he wanted to make the strongest possible case
for the Directory's continued support of his costly Italian
campaign, he spoke exclusively in the language of business.

If you want to make your stakeholders hear you as clearly
as Napoleon made the Directory hear him, speak in the only
language they want to hear: money out and money in, money
lost and money made.

■

Lesson 126
Work the Magic of Morale

> "[My soldiers] are playing and laughing with death. . . .
> [T]hey sing in turn of country and love."
> ~Letter to the Directory during the Italian Campaign, June 1, 1796

Napoleon's brand of warfare was hard. Not only did he require the
utmost degree of offensive aggression—attacks characterized by
extreme violence—but he brought his army into the positions to
make those attacks by means of relentless forced marches. Especially during his early campaigns, his armies were often short on
everything needful: food, clothing, weapons, and manpower. Soldiers had every reason to despair. Morale should have been in crisis.
Instead, Napoleon made morale the fulcrum on which he raised his
armies to victory, beginning with the chronically underfed, under-
supplied Army of Italy.

This has seemed to many historians like magic—the inexplic-
able product of Napoleon's extraordinary charisma. To those who

served under Napoleon, however, the magic was indeed present, but its sources were practical rather than mystical. The morale that made his soldiers play and laugh with death had four clear sources:

1. Napoleon shared the life, dangers, and fate of his soldiers. He was always in the battle, not leading it from afar. He mingled with his troops so freely that, during the Italian campaign, they dubbed him the "little corporal," an affectionate and admiring sobriquet that stuck to him throughout his military career.

2. Napoleon empowered his soldiers by connecting them to his endeavors and giving them a stake in the outcome of the hardships and hazards they were undertaking. He told his troops what they had to achieve, why they had to achieve it, and what benefits their achievements would have for their country (which Napoleon expressed in terms of the soldiers' families) and for themselves (a combination of glory and plunder).

3. Napoleon promised his soldiers a better future. He admitted that conditions were bad for them in the present, and he used this fact to motivate them by persuading them that they (and only they) possessed the skill, might, courage, and will to create—under his leadership—that future.

4. Napoleon produced results. He led his soldiers to one victory after another. He persuaded them that they were partners in victory, that, together, they could not be defeated. He not only celebrated each victory with his soldiers, he addressed them to ensure that they understood the magnitude of each achievement and the role they had played in it.

Morale works magic, but morale is built on the most basic of emotions—confidence in a clear and worthwhile purpose, faith in competent leadership, satisfaction in being rewarded for achievement, freedom from fear of betrayal, and the repeated joy of repeated triumph. If you would create an enterprise pervaded by the highest morale—the level of morale that brings success—you must consistently create the conditions that satisfy all of these emotional needs.

■

Lesson 127
Find the Courage of Tomorrow

> "The fortunes of war are changeable, my dear general; we shall retrieve tomorrow or the day after what you have lost today. . . . Nothing is lost as long as courage remains."
> ~Message to General André Masséna, July 29, 1796

At three in the morning on July 29, 1796, Napoleon was awakened with news that a surprise Austrian attack had driven back the forces of one of his most trusted generals, André Masséna, thereby threatening the important French-held city of Verona. At the same time, another surprise attack had forced another of his generals into retreat.

Bad news delivered at three in the morning is a powerful inducement to panic. Napoleon, who coined the phrase "two o'clock in the morning courage" to describe one indispensable prerequisite of a commander, drew on that commodity now. He dashed off a dispatch to Masséna, explaining that what was lost on one occasion would be "retrieved" on another, provided that courage remained.

He did not leave his general with these words alone, but gave him as well a series of concrete orders designed to minimize further loss and put him in a position to recover: "burn your bridge," he ordered (this would delay the enemy's pursuit), "reorganize your force; fall back a little tonight . . . [then] Fall back on the Mincio [river] but cover Castelnovo . . . where I shall be shortly after midnight [tomorrow]."

For Napoleon, courage did not consist in a hollow display of bravado, but was a vision that allowed a general to see beyond defeat, to overcome the fear that any particular loss was irretrievable and final. Courage was the force that carried an army into tomorrow. The emphasis on courage was the most important part of Napoleon's message, but it rested on the firm ground of specific actions needed to preserve "tomorrow" as a platform from which courage could launch a new effort.

Courage is the fuel of hope. It is not fearlessness. It is not bluster. It is not contained in a battle cry. Courage is less about facing defeat or even enduring defeat than it is about taking you and your organization past defeat. No commodity, no force, no source is more valuable than courage properly understood. You must understand it, possess it, cultivate it, and, above all, share it with those you lead.

■

Lesson 128
Pass the Credit

"It is said that the Roman legions marched twenty-four miles a day; our brigades have marched thirty while also fighting."
~Letter to the Directory, January 18, 1797

Napoleon's victory at the Second Battle of Rivoli in January 1797 positioned him for his final triumph in the first Italian campaign. He knew he would be hailed as his country's savior, and he was determined to make the most of his victory. For him, that meant sharing rather than claiming the credit.

Often condemned by contemporaries and historians alike as an egomaniac, Napoleon actually indulged in remarkably little self-aggrandizement. Instead, he was always generous in apportioning the credit for victories to his generals and to the men of his armies. What is more, he did so in communications built of verbs and nouns rather than adverbs and adjectives. He marshaled the facts much as he marshaled his troops, and he let the facts fight the battle of public relations. His January 18, 1797, dispatch to the Directory was typical: He cited the legendary endurance of the Roman Legions, with their twenty-four-mile-a-day marches (and he was careful to give the precise figure), only to put the achievement of his own men above theirs. They made *thirty*-mile *fighting* marches.

Modesty? Of course not. Generosity? Yes—though hardly selfless.

Giving due credit to his army was, after all, giving due credit to *his* army. For, by this time, the Army of Italy had become universally identified as *Napoleon's army,* and, as he well knew, a general is only as good as his army. Sharing the credit amplified the credit, revealing Napoleon not merely as a "military genius" but as a maker of supermen. He must have known that if people could see him as a forger of invincible armies, they would have little trouble envisioning him as a leader of nations and, of course, as *their* leader.

Contrary to what common sense might suggest, sharing credit for an achievement that you have led does not dilute the benefit to you but concentrates it and makes it far more potent. Your personal achievements mean nothing to others unless those others benefit from your achievements even more than you do. Share the credit, because doing so builds morale and motivates even greater achievement, and because it is the right thing to do. But, most of all, share the credit because it will make your triumph relevant to every other stakeholder in the enterprise.

Acclaim is valueless until you start to give it away.

Lesson 129
Make Them See Your Strategy

> "You are going to undertake a conquest of which the effects on world civilization and commerce will be incalculable. You will give England the most positive and painful blow before delivering the death blow."
>
> ~Address to soldiers, June 22, 1798, quoted in Robert Asprey,
> *The Rise of Napoleon Bonaparte*, 2000

Napoleon proposed to haul an army halfway around the world to fight in Egypt. He understood that this required an explanation. And so, in an age in which soldiers were universally expected never to reason why but simply to do and die, Napoleon not only gave his troops an explanation, but even shared his strategy with them.

The French conquest of Egypt, he explained, would have profound long-term effects on civilization and commerce, but the more immediate object of these effects was to destroy once and for all the nation every soldier, no matter how uninformed, knew as the implacable and eternal enemy of France: England. By blocking English ambitions in Egypt, France would not only control this important crossroads between Europe, Africa, and Asia Minor, it would perch on India's doorstep, ready to wrest that prize from English hands. By defeating England's outposts of empire, France would curb its rival forever, reducing England to an insular power no longer able to pose a military or commercial threat.

The Egyptian campaign was extravagant and ultimately unrealistic, yet Napoleon won acceptance for it from the Directory as well as from his own generals and troops. He did so by explaining this most exotic enterprise in the most familiar terms, as yet another campaign against an anciently familiar enemy.

Intelligent and informed compliance is always preferable to dumb obedience. To the degree that doing so is compatible with security concerns, share your strategy with those whose job it is to execute it. Make them see how they fit in. Show them that they are indispensable to the grand design. Make that grand design relevant to their lives and their success.

■

Lesson 130
Manage the Message

"If the press is not bridled, I shall not remain three days in power."

~Remark made shortly after Napoleon's elevation to first consul, quoted in Felix Markham, *Napoleon*, 1963

As first consul—virtual dictator of post-revolutionary France—Napoleon acted immediately to seize control of the press. In January 1800, for example, he issued a decree suppressing sixty of Paris's seventy-three political journals. One of the jobs of Napoleon's secretary, Louis Antoine Fauvelet de Bourrienne, was to read aloud key international papers as his master was being shaved in the morning.

"Skip it, skip it," Napoleon would say when Bourrienne began to read from the French papers. "I know what is in them. They only say what I tell them to."

Napoleon made it a top priority to control the French press. The only voice he wanted Frenchmen to hear was his own. Such extreme censorship would, of course, be intolerable in a modern democratic society, and the United States and other democracies have always valued a free press. Likewise, no CEO of even a modest-sized company would long survive if she actively suppressed voices other than her own. We value transparency, and we value freedom of expression. For that matter, only in an organization that honors such values can a leader find credible—because unforced—endorsement.

This said, no CEO will long survive if she relinquishes control of her message.

As a leader, you own what Theodore Roosevelt called a "bully pulpit." This does not give you the license to suppress open communication within your organization, but it does confer a great advantage for the delivery of *your* message above and in preference to the messages of others. Fail to use this advantage frequently, consistently, and effectively, and you will surrender it, thereby conceding credibility and authority to other messages and other messengers.

Your job is not to *control* everything that is said within the organization (although you can and should exercise considerable control over what is communicated to the outside from within) but to actively *manage* the message. You have the platform as well as the responsibility to do so.

■

Lesson 131
Offer Baubles

> "You are pleased to call them [awards and honors created by Napoleon] 'baubles'; well, it is with 'baubles' that mankind is governed."
>
> ~Remark made probably to Antoine Thibaudeau,
> ex-revolutionary, 1802, quoted in
> Felix Markham, *Napoleon*, 1963

After Napoleon was elevated to first consul—essentially, absolute dictator of France—he created a "Legion of Honor" with an array of hierarchical ranks replete with decorations and lucrative pensions to be awarded to deserving and influential men. Napoleon saw this scheme as a means of recognizing genuine achievement, to be sure, but it would also serve as way of making him the central source of all patronage, thereby ensuring the personal loyalty of the men he made powerful.

Reportedly, when the radical-leaning, reform-minded ex-revolutionary Antoine Thibaudeau objected to Napoleon's unseemly creation of what he denigrated as mere "baubles," the First Consul made no denial, but instead asserted their sovereign motivational potency.

No one valued and honored genuine achievement more highly than Napoleon. Yet while he appreciated accomplishment for its intrinsic value, he was also quick to attach external value to it in ways that would ensure his own establishment at the top. Management manuals advise bosses to recognize and reward employee achievement because doing so is good for the morale of the organization and reinforces a high level of performance and productivity. These are very good reasons for creating an incentive system, but, as Napoleon understood, honors and rewards—especially financial rewards—also serve to build the leader's power and influence by continually reinforcing the loyalty of the members of the organization. To those who thought this approach cynical, Napoleon offered no rebuttal other than to point out (in effect) that the efficient order of any truly successful enterprise is built on such systems—even at the risk of cynicism.

■

Lesson 132
Give Everybody the Hope of Rising

> "Equality in the sense that everyone will be master—there you
> have the secret of all your vanities. What must be done, therefore,
> is to give everybody the hope of being able to rise."
>
> ~ Conversation from about 1802, quoted in
> Felix Markham, *Napoleon*, 1963

Napoleon was no mere military conqueror, but thought long and deeply about the nature of government, especially in the post-revolutionary climate of France. He believed that, for most Frenchmen, the concept of equality had less to do with the general leveling of society than it did with a desire that everyman would be a master. Napoleon held that this attitude was ultimately a "vanity"—an empty belief—and yet he was resolved to use the attitude as a way of motivating loyalty, compliance, and high levels of performance. If everyone aspired to be a master, Napoleon resolved to "give everybody the hope of being able to rise."

On the face of it, this seems a cynical and self-serving policy. But look deeper. Napoleon sincerely believed in creating a government and a military based on merit: a meritocracy. "My motto has always been," he famously remarked in 1815 while exiled on St. Helena, "a career open to all talents, without distinction of birth." Certainly, his own rise from humble origins on the political and social backwater of Corsica was a case in point to validate the notion of meritocracy. And while Napoleon often appointed men to high political office on the basis of political patronage or their blood relationship to himself, he built the high command of his armies very much according to merit as measured by victories delivered.

Many leaders voice their belief in merit as a motive for promotion through the ranks of an organization, but all too many regard meritocracy passively, assuming that the cream will naturally float to the top. The truth is that merit must be actively recognized—sought, cultivated, and rewarded to ensure that the most capable people come to occupy positions of responsibility and leadership. At the same time, everyone must be given the hope—the rational, credible hope—of rising. The leaders of the organization must talk about merit as a highly valued principle, and they must ensure that their words are never in conflict with reality. The organization must truly operate as a meritocracy, in which achievement is actively, consistently, and visibly rewarded and the most capable, most experienced, and most productive individuals are promoted to positions of influence and power. If the offer of hope has no correlative in the reality of the organization, the offer and those who make it will be written off as cynical and manipulative. Allow this to happen, and the morale, commitment, loyalty, and productivity of the enterprise will erode at a rate both astounding and appalling.

■

Lesson 133
Set the Tone

> "The first moments [of a battle] are apt to be the most lively and
> decisive. You must set the tone for the officers."
> ~Letter to General Auguste-Frédéric-Louis Marmont,
> March 12, 1804

A general is officially authorized to issue orders and, by military law, his orders must be obeyed. This is important, but Napoleon recognized that it is only a fraction of what actually constitutes leadership.

Whatever authority a leader may claim by rank, title, or official decree, his most compelling power as a commander is not imposed on the members of the army but bestowed by them. To earn his authority, the commander must set the "tone" for his subordinate officers and, indeed, for the entire army. *Tone* is not a product of orders, much less threats of punishment or even promises of reward. It is an impression created day by day and hour by hour, an impression that the general is truly in command—that he is the master of the situation, that he is intimately familiar with every aspect of his army, that he possesses the vision to lead it, and that he cares about the welfare of his officers and men. It is the product of policy and action and the result of leadership by deed and example.

Tone is the image and feeling a leader creates in the hearts and minds of those he leads. Napoleon knew that it could not be faked and that it had to be created continuously and consistently, transmitted through everything the general said and did.

> **Do not look** to your professional title, corporate rank, or job description for leadership authority. The right to lead is given, not taken. Set a tone in your organization that will prompt the members of the enterprise to volunteer to you the right to lead.

■

Lesson 134
The Eye of the Commander

> "The eye of the commander must remedy everything."
> ~Letter to Rear Admiral Carel Hendrik Ver Huell, May 21, 1804

Unless they continually feel the "presence of the commander," subordinate officers, "whatever their merits might be in other respects," are in a "state of carelessness," Napoleon wrote.

Napoleon required a general to be everywhere or, at the very least, give his command the impression that he was ubiquitous. He demanded that his top commanders survey everything, so that they could detect problems wherever they might crop up and instantly remedy them. But in writing of the "eye of the commander" he meant more than simply requiring generals to diligently oversee their commands. He intended for generals to act and speak in ways that always and everywhere made *their presence felt,* whether they were physically on the scene or not.

An army must sense the presence of the all-seeing eye of the commander. Developing this degree of "command presence" (to use a modern term of military art) requires the continuous communication of values and expectations. It also requires creating the impression that the commander is not only in unbroken contact with his command, but that he shares its fate. And it requires, above all, that the general impress his personality on the entire army, that every officer and enlisted soldier identify himself with the commander.

Soldiers who fought under Napoleon never spoke of themselves as troops of the French army, but soldiers of *Napoleon's army.* They felt themselves to be continually under his eye.

To lose contact with your organization is fatal to leadership. Develop "command presence" by continually manifesting and demonstrating your presence to the enterprise. Get out of your office. Show yourself everywhere as often as possible. Talk to employees at all levels—or, more to the point, *listen* to them. In all communications with your organization, emphasize your values and expectations. Share your personality with the group. Impress yourself on the people who, after all, *are* the company. Become the all-seeing, ever-present "eye" of your enterprise.

■

Lesson 135
Paycheck Players

"They recruit only for money."

~ Letter to Minister of Police Joseph Fouché, August 6, 1805

Napoleon faulted the British for recruiting soldiers "only for money" and pointed out that they compounded this error by also emptying "their prisons into their regiments." Recruited for money or as an alternative to incarceration, British soldiers lacked loyalty, patriotism, and all other positive motivation, Napoleon explained in a letter to Joseph Fouché. He then went on to present an analysis of the failure of *esprit* in the British army:

1. Absent positive reasons for service, the British army was held together by "cruel" discipline, which further alienated the troops, making them wholly unreliable.

2. Because they are unreliable, the ranks of the British army produced mediocre (or worse) noncommissioned officers.

3. Because the noncommissioned ranks were chronically inadequate, the British were forced to "increase the number of officers beyond all proportion," making for an expensive, inefficient, top-heavy force—especially since officer commissions were bought and sold in the British military system.

What Napoleon described in the British army, any modern sportswriter would recognize as "paycheck players": team members who work for nothing more than money. Staffing any competitive enterprise with paycheck players is a false economy that presents a weak value proposition. Hire thoughtlessly or cheaply at the bottom, and you will pay for it at the top—in excessive management costs, a work product of poor quality, and countless other inefficiencies. Always build from the bottom up.

Lesson 136
Provide Vital Latitude

> "This letter is the principal instruction for your plan of campaign, and if unforeseen events should occur, you will be guided in your conduct by the spirit of the instruction."
>
> ~Letter from Marshal Louis-Alexandre Berthier to General Gouvion St. Cyr, passing on Napoleon's instructions for the Ulm campaign, September 1805

Napoleon gave highly detailed instructions to his commanders for carrying out all campaigns, but what he added in the case of the Ulm campaign in September 1805 is of more than passing interest. He made explicit a certain degree of latitude in contemplating the unforeseen, instructing his commanders to abide by the spirit, not necessarily the letter, of his instructions.

Napoleon ascribed little value to absolute obedience. Instead, his objective was to elicit compliance with the spirit of his orders by giving his commanders sufficient space to use their own judgment in the case of unforeseen events and the exigencies that are associated with any battle.

Effective real-world leadership must make allowances for the real world. Instructions can be cut and dried, but events more than often are not. Create instructions that provide latitude for the managers on the ground to cope with the unforeseen. Emphasize the spirit of your instructions rather than the letter. Blind obedience to instructions rendered irrelevant by reality is a sure route to catastrophe.

Lesson 137
Be a Great Communicator

> "Seizing the essential point of subjects, stripping them of useless
> accessories, developing his thought and never ceasing to elaborate
> it till he had made it perfectly clear and conclusive, always finding
> the fitting word for the thing, or inventing one where the image of
> language had not created it, [Napoleon's] conversation was ever
> full of interest. . . . Yet he did not fail to listen to the remarks and
> objections which were addressed to him . . . and I have never felt
> the least difficulty in saying to him what I believed to be the truth,
> even when it was not likely to please him."
>
> ~Prince von Metternich, on dealing with Napoleon,
> quoted in Felix Markham, *Napoleon*, 1963

Considered the most powerful diplomat of his age, Klemens Wenzel, Prince von Metternich (1773–1859), served as Austria's ambassador to France from 1806 to 1809. It was a period during which he often spoke with Napoleon, and his description of the man in conversation is a concise enumeration of what it takes to be a leader-communicator. Metternich depicts Napoleon as:

1. An incisive analyst, with a gift for penetrating to the heart of a subject.

2. A communicator who first stripped all nonessentials from the core issues, then, on this concentrated foundation, built his thoughts.

3. Relentless in his quest for clarity.

4. Relentless in his quest to arrive at a decisive conclusion.

5. Scrupulous in the use of precise language.

6. Innovative in his quest for precisely the right word.

7. An acute listener.

8. Open to whatever he was told.

9. An asker of questions.

10. Able to dispute without becoming obnoxious in his disputation.

11. Able to disagree and refuse without alienating his partners in conversation.

12. Able to make any conversation businesslike.

13. A facilitator of dialog.

14. Willing to hear the truth, even if it was unpleasant.

Study Prince Metternich's description of Napoleon the leader-communicator. Every quality Metternich noted is worthy of faithful emulation.

■

Lesson 138
Attend to the Human Details

"Write to Corporal Bernaudet of the 13th of the Line and tell him not to drink so much and to behave better. He has been given the Cross [of the Legion of Honor] because he is a brave man. One must not take it away from him because he is a bit fond of wine. Make him understand, however, that he is wrong to get into a state which brings shame on the decoration he wears."

~Letter to the chancellor of the Legion of Honor, May 1807

No detail seemed to escape Napoleon, especially one bearing on character, performance, or morale. For the supreme commander to show concern for a mere corporal would be astounding in any army at any time. In Napoleon's day, it was unheard of. General Auguste-Frédéric-Louis Marmont believed that, through "familiarities of this kind [Napoleon] made the soldiers adore him, but," he added, "it was a means only available to a commander whom frequent victories had made illustrious; any other general would have injured his reputation by it."

Cultivating an effective leadership image requires a willingness to engage everyone on a warm, respectful, human level by showing interest in them and by remembering the human details important to them, including names of family members, outside interests, and so on. Yet it is not sufficient to be "one of the guys." A record of "frequent victories"—success—is essential to the leadership formula.

■

Lesson 139
Can You Buy Good Behavior?

> "My intention is to make the Generals so rich that I shall never
> hear of them dishonoring by cupidity the most noble profession,
> and attract the contempt of the soldiers."
>
> ~Letter to Joseph Bonaparte from 1808, quoted
> in Felix Markham, *Napoleon*, 1963

Napoleon believed honor, glory, patriotism, and public service were great motivators, but he was also convinced that sealing the deal required cash and plenty of it. He was steeped in what a later age would call *realpolitik*—"real" as opposed to "ideal" politics—and concluded that "cupidity" (we might say *avarice* or *greed*) was the most reliable motivational force of all.

Although he was condemned by many as a tyrant, Napoleon actually sought to give as many people as possible a tangible stake in the success of his leadership. The more powerful his subordinates, he reasoned, the more useful they were to him—but also (in his view) the more dangerous. To mitigate this hazard,

Napoleon gave them a larger and more tangible stake in the enterprise.

To Napoleon, the purchase of loyalty and good behavior, while possibly distasteful, seemed both inevitable and self-evident. In the long run, however, it was perhaps the least successful aspect of his leadership policy. Showering his generals with wealth stimulated rather than appeased their appetite for extravagance. Instead of warding off moral corruption, it accelerated it. Instead of attaching the generals to him as their leader, Napoleon's bounty served to attach the generals only to themselves. It was, in the end, a self-defeating approach to leadership that created the very problems it was intended to prevent.

Among the generals Napoleon made rich, François Joseph Lefebvre, for whom he created the title of duke of Dantzig, was among the most fabulously wealthy. Nevertheless, at Napoleon's fall in 1814, the duke piped up: "Did he believe that when we have titles, honors, and lands, we will kill ourselves for his sake?"

The principle of reward commensurate with the value one offers is deeply ingrained not only in our capitalist society, but also in human nature itself. People perceive a value-for-value exchange as just, and any manager who fails to reward value with equivalent value cannot hope to sustain, let alone grow, his organization. Yet while money is an essential vehicle for conveying fair value in a business relationship, it is also a value in itself, independent of you and your enterprise. Anyone with means can offer more money than you and your organization; therefore, a relationship built exclusively on material rewards connects the employee to the cash, not the company.

In the end, you have to offer more than money, and what you offer must be a value intrinsic to you and your organization. What kinds of values connect people to companies? When people are asked, they answer with such phrases as *meaningful work, ethical work, worthwhile work, a chance to make a differ-ence, the opportunity to help others, inspiring work,* and *learning new things.* The cash reward is indispensable, but not sufficient—not for the people in your organization and not for you as a leader of the enterprise.

■

Lesson 140
Everyone a Rifleman

"The officers . . . could carry carbines to set the example."
~ Letter to Intendant General Pierre-Antoine Daru,
March 27, 1808

In the armies of Napoleon's day, only enlisted combat troops carried muskets or rifles (enlisted cavalrymen carried light, short-barreled rifles called *carbines*). Officers were armed only with sabers and, sometimes, pistols, whereas transport troops, who handled and drove the baggage train, were either unarmed or carried only pistols. To transform his armies into instruments of total war, Napoleon introduced what was in the early nineteenth century the radical concept of making every man a rifleman. He ordered carbines to be issued to transport soldiers and even to officers. "I do not see why the teamsters of a convoy . . . should not join the escort in defending their wagons," Napoleon wrote.

Give everyone in your organization some role in the main business of the organization. Avoid separating operations into a "front office" and "back office" or into "production" and "support." Everyone should have an active, even urgent stake in the firm's existence. Everyone should feel responsible for generating revenue, for making a profit, and for creating value. Hand everyone a rifle.

■

Lesson 141
Create Group Identity

> "Establish a basic distinction between marching and provisional
> regiments in Spain. A provisional regiment . . . is organized and
> must not undergo any change while it remains in Spain. A
> marching regiment . . . is a temporary organization for the pur-
> pose of conducting troops to the provisional regiments. . . . [The]
> army is formed only through constant care and you must not
> depart from this policy."
>
> ~ Letter to Marshal Jean-Baptiste Bessières, April 16, 1808

Napoleon left the prosecution of the Spanish campaign to his subordinate marshal and generals, but nevertheless inundated them with a
steady flow of instructions in what turned out to be a vain effort to compensate for his physical absence. Of particular concern to him was the
maintenance of the army as something more than a mere body of
armed men. He sought to introduce stability into the force by creating
so-called provisional regiments, which, though established specifically
to fight in Spain, were given permanent organizational status, as if they
had been long established. The idea was to promote among the individual soldiers and officers effective group identification and *esprit de
corps*. To ensure the stability of these organizations, Napoleon created
separate "marching regiments," which were ad hoc military formations
intended to do no more than maintain good order among soldiers en
route to assignment in one of the provisional regiments. By transferring
men in distinct groups from the marching regiments to the provisional
regiments rather than piecemeal, Napoleon sought to preserve the insti-
tutional quality of the provisional regiments. An army that loses its *esprit*
becomes a disorderly and demoralized mob.

Promote a group identity within your team, department, or
company. Most of us derive strength and inspiration from
feeling that we are a part of something both worthwhile and

bigger than ourselves. If you allow your enterprise to appear as if it is equipped with a revolving door or staffed by transients and squatters, you will lose many of the synergistic benefits of corporate and collaborative organization.

∎

Lesson 142
Be Indispensable

"In war men are nothing; one man is everything."
~ "Notes on the Affairs in Spain," August 30, 1808, quoted in
Jay Luvaas, *Napoleon on the Art of War*, 1999

Napoleon declared "the presence of the general" to be "indispensable." The general "is the head, the whole of an army"; the Roman Legions did not subdue Gaul, Caesar did. "An army is nothing without the head."

For Napoleon, the general was the visionary, the planner, and the decision maker. He was the head of the army, its brains. He was the absolute leader, the author of the battle and the war.

In these very literal ways, the general was indispensable. Yet Napoleon did not express himself quite this way. His declaration was not "The general is indispensable," but *"The presence of the general is indispensable."* The distinction between the two assertions is a crucial one. For the concept of *presence* suggests something deeper than the planning and deciding roles of the general. Vitally important as these are, it is the way the leader presents himself—how he manifests himself to those he leads—that Napoleon emphasizes most emphatically. To this day, U.S. Army officers in training hear countless lectures on "command presence"—the look, the gestures, the attitude, and the vocabulary through which a leader conveys her leadership and either makes it stick or fails to.

"Command presence" is essential to leadership. It is first and foremost about *being present,* which means earning your right to leadership in everything you do and say. Command is not a role to be played occasionally. It must live in your heart and find expression in every interchange with your enterprise. It is not a uniform, but a second skin. Its elements can be learned, but they must be practiced so thoroughly as to become second nature. To be indispensable requires understanding that you cannot afford even a moment of absence. Like Caesar—like Napoleon—you must be the organization you lead.

Lesson 143
Teach Against Surrender

> "Clearly convey the notion that [an officer commanding a detached, isolated column] must never give up all hope, that if surrounded he must not surrender."
>
> ~ Letter to General Henri-Jacques-Guillaume Clarke,
> October 1, 1809

Napoleon wanted cadets at the celebrated St. Cyr military academy to learn certain basics. Among these were the rules of encamping, the duties of a commander of an infantry column, and so on. Of greatest importance to him was conveying the notion that an officer in command of a wholly detached and therefore isolated unit must not give up hope when surrounded and must not surrender except "under the butt end of muskets." He advised compiling and presenting historical examples of isolated columns that found ways to break out of envelopments "by making the most of all their resources and their courage."

Napoleon was not interested in soldiers fighting to the death. Dead soldiers were of no use to him. Yet he was convinced, however, that "he who prefers death to ignominy saves himself and lives with honor, while . . . the man who prefers life dies by covering himself with shame." He advised General Clarke to see to it that both ancient and modern histories were gleaned for examples of this apparently paradoxical truth, and that these be presented to cadets as the standard of conduct for a soldier of France.

> **Make giving up** harder to do than persevering against the odds. Create an environment in which surrender—walking away—is unthinkable. Do this through education. Expose the members of your organization to examples of victory in abundance. Banish stories of capitulation. Create and share a group history in which perseverance emerges as the norm rather than the exception.

■

Lesson 144
Developing Human Assets

> "It must be at one and the same time a work of science and history. The narrative sometimes must even be entertaining. It should stimulate interest, contain details, and if necessary have plans added to it. But it must not . . . be over the heads of . . . the young men."
>
> ~ Letter to General Henri-Jacques-Guillaume Clarke,
> October 1, 1809

Thus Napoleon described to his minister of war the specifications for a new training manual. He considered such a text of "great importance," and he promised that its author would be "well rewarded."

As a leader of soldiers, Napoleon might have simply insisted that it was the duty of his troops to learn. Instead, he was determined to motivate and to facilitate their learning—to make the curriculum compelling, even entertaining, capable of stimulating interest, and sufficiently detailed to be genuinely useful, but pitched perfectly at the intellectual level of the student. He was especially insistent that the text combine science (theory) with history (what actually happened). The two branches of inquiry, Napoleon believed, were essential to understanding anything of real significance. The one could not meaningfully stand without the other.

Develop the human assets of your organization through mentoring, instruction, and other education. You will be tempted simply to spoon-feed instruction (most training programs do precisely this), but it is a mistake to expect employees to learn just because they are being paid to do so. Make the lessons meaningful and compelling. Embody them in a narrative that invites the student in, that makes her a part of the story. Balance theory with practice—"science with history"—and engage the student at her level. In this way, build understanding.

■

Lesson 145
Demand, Support, and Reward Energy

> "You are commander in chief; you must remove all difficulties."
> ~Letter to Marshal Jean-Baptiste Bessières, November 20, 1809

Jean-Baptiste Bessières was one of Napoleon's most successful marshals, and late in 1809 he was enjoying success opposing the British Walcheren expedition in the Netherlands despite an epidemic of malaria—popularly called "Walcheren Fever"—that plagued both sides. The ill health of many of Bessières's troops doubtless contributed to Napoleon's criticism that the marshal was failing to "march with suitable energy." If so, Napoleon preempted any excuse Bessières might have offered based on Walcheren Fever by telling him that as commander in chief, his job was to "remove all difficulties."

He instructed Bessières to "March rapidly and vigorously without any *but, if,* or *because.* Overcome all obstacles."

If Napoleon's demand brooked no excuses, the support he offered was also unconditional. He not only expressed what he called his "special affection" for Bessières, explaining that it had moved him to assign the marshal the special privilege of acquiring the glory that would flow from the mission in Walcheren, but promised that he would "disapprove your actions only if they are faint-hearted and irresolute. Everything that is vigorous, firm, and discreet will meet with my approval."

> **You have the** right and the obligation to require maximum effort and wholehearted, high-energy commitment from your organization. Those on whom you call to perform at this level have, in turn, the right and the obligation to require your absolute support for their full-on effort. All business is an exchange of value for value. You cannot demand value if you do not intend to give value in return. The support and reward you offer must be human as well as monetary—that is, it must include respect, gratitude, and what Napoleon called "special affection."

■

Lesson 146
Make It Happen

"Give your orders in such a way that they cannot be disobeyed."
~Letter to Marshal Louis-Alexandre Berthier, March 29, 1811

Ship's captains in the navies of Napoleon's day traditionally appended the imperative sentence "Make it so" to the orders they issued. The message was not so much "obey me" as it was *give reality the shape I have ordered,* and the implied meaning was to achieve this by doing whatever had to be done. Although Napoleon was a land soldier and notoriously deficient when it came to naval matters, his understanding of military orders was precisely along the lines of *make it so*. While he believed that a subordinate was obligated to question an order he did not understand, considered mistaken, or deemed immoral, Napoleon also held that all lawful orders were to be obeyed absolutely, fully, and without reservation. This imposed an obligation on the recipient of the order, of course—failure to carry out an order was (Napoleon declared) a "crime and . . . must be punished"—but also on its issuer.

Napoleon advised composing an order so that it could not be disobeyed. This meant creating crystal clear instructions and explaining them as necessary. The purpose and the logic of the order needed to be made clear. Although a subordinate was legally obliged to follow an order, Napoleon believed in securing a level of understanding that was likely to produce enthusiastic and energetic execution. He wanted subordinates to buy into all that his vision and will directed.

Your orders, instructions, and directives must be unambiguous. They must be designed to create understanding, agreement, and enthusiasm in addition to total and efficient compliance. Emulate Napoleon's refusal to rely on simple rules requiring obedience and, like him, construct orders that appeal to the intelligence and judgment of those required to execute them. Informed voluntary compliance is always preferable to reflexive compulsion.

■

Lesson 147
Value Experience

> "We need men and not boys."
> ~Letter to General Henri-Jacques-Guillaume Clarke,
> October 15, 1813

Napoleon believed that no one was braver than "our" French boys, but "lacking [the physical] fortitude [of mature men] they fill the hospitals and even at the slightest uncertainty they show the character of their age." Eighteen-year-olds, Napoleon believed, were too young to wage war, but not too young to be trained, clothed, armed, and drilled—prepared for combat service at the age of twenty-two to twenty-four. Even troops of this age, he wrote, should be mixed with older veterans in the field so that they would take a liking to military service.

Napoleon did not believe in using soldiers as cannon fodder. Every man had to count. Useless soldiers, men who did nothing more than fill vacant spaces, not only got themselves wounded or killed, they had to be fed and supplied without providing value. A useful soldier had to be trained and drilled, then, when reasonably mature, schooled on the field of battle, transformed from raw recruit into seasoned veteran. The process required an investment of time, manpower, and money, and, because it was an investment, it had to be protected. In an era during which soldiers were treated as an expendable commodity—buried in mass graves, their very bones often sold to be ground up into fertilizer—Napoleon advocated doing everything necessary to "encourage soldiers . . . to remain with the colors." This would be done by recognizing and rewarding seniority, with honors and with cash. "It is a great injustice not to pay a veteran more than a recruit," he believed, and good soldiers will tolerate all manner of hardship, but they will turn in anger and disgust from injustice.

Don't hire empty suits. Invest the time and energy required to select the right people, then invest in them, cultivate them, take care of them, reward them, and keep them. As the soldier is the army, a business is its people.

■

Lesson 148
Create Self-Sufficiency

> "A general should never put his army into cantonments when he has the means of collecting supplies of forage and provisions, and of thus providing for the wants of the soldier in the field."
>
> ~ Military Maxim LV

Camp life had a demoralizing effect on the soldiers of Napoleon's era. Boredom and idleness tended to erode discipline. Moreover, adequate sanitation was often difficult to provide and maintain, making cantonments breeding grounds for disease, which posed a greater threat to armies than any human enemy. Finally, encampments always provided an inviting target for raids and attacks. For these reasons, Napoleon believed soldiers should be made to live off the land wherever possible. This not only made good economic sense, it instilled in troops a self-sufficiency that was conducive to discipline, order, and initiative.

Cultivate, encourage, and reward self-sufficiency throughout your organization. Consider performance-based compensation or systems of performance-based bonuses. Give each member of the enterprise a personal stake in creating its success on a daily basis.

■

Lesson 149
To Be a Motivator

> "It is not set speeches at the moment of battle that render soldiers
> brave. The veteran scarcely listens to them, and the recruit forgets
> them at the first discharge [of gunfire]. If discourses and harangues
> are useful, it is during the campaign . . . to do away with unfavor-
> able impressions, to correct false reports, to keep alive a proper
> spirit in the camp, and to furnish materials and amusement for the
> bivouac. All printed orders of the day should keep in view these
> objects."
>
> ~Military Maxim LXI

Popular mythology portrays Napoleon, the skirts of his long gray
greatcoat windswept on some hill, delivering a stirring speech of
encouragement and inspiration to his adoring soldiers. There is
some truth to this picture. In contrast to many high commanders of
this period, who held themselves aloof from their troops—a matter
of social class more than command style—Napoleon frequently
walked among his men, spoke with them, and addressed them. He
did frequently remind them that they were "soldiers of France" and
that much was therefore expected of them, but he rarely delivered
"set speeches" focused on patriotic glory. Instead, he did something
truly radical for a commander speaking to his army, whether in 1800
or in more recent times. He told them the truth.

He told them the truth—as he saw it.

He explained the mission at hand. He explained the overall
objectives of the army. He especially sought to counter "unfavorable impressions" and "false reports" with the information he
wanted his officers and men to have. He countered pessimism—the
prevailing mood of virtually all camp gossip—with optimism. No
objective historian who reads the campaign accounts Napoleon
sent to the Directory can fail to see that Napoleon was often optimistic well beyond what the objective facts of a situation warranted;
however, this optimism was the truth of his perception rather than

a deliberate distortion or lie. Napoleon's genius lay in his uncanny capacity to bring reality into line with his most extravagantly optimistic vision of it. By delivering *his* version of reality to *his* soldiers, he sought "to keep alive a proper spirit in the camp." Note that Napoleon did not rely exclusively on his personal presence to transmit the desired messages to the troops, but called for the "printed orders of the day" to publish facts and other necessary information.

Want to inspire your "troops"? Communicate on a regular basis. Deliver two key items of information: first, your vision of reality as it is and, second, your version of reality as you want it to become. Both must be credible, yet both should clearly bear the stamp of your leadership. You should not even pretend to sell them to the enterprise as objective transcripts of the real world. Paint your picture of reality clearly, vividly, and believably. Inspire your "troops" to transform your vision into reality.

■

Lesson 150
Abide No Rogues

"There is no security for any sovereign, for any nation, or for any general, if officers are permitted to capitulate in the open field, and to lay down their arms in virtue of conditions favorable to the contracting party, but contrary to the interests of the army at large. To withdraw from danger, and thereby to involve their comrades in greater peril, is the height of cowardice. Such conduct should be proscribed, declared infamous, and made punishable with death. All generals, officers, and soldiers who capitulate in battle to save their own lives should be decimated.

"He who gives the order and those who obey are alike traitors,
and deserve capital punishment."

~ Military Maxim LXVIII

During the full maturity of his military career, Napoleon often
commanded vast armies numbering well into the six figures and
requiring the services of hundreds of officers, any one of whom
had the potential power to lead his company, battalion, regiment,
or corps into a separate peace with the enemy "in virtue of conditions favorable to the contracting party, but contrary to the interests of the army at large." The only means Napoleon could con-
ceive to discourage such self-interested capitulations was to ensure
that they were rendered virtually unthinkable by branding them as
the height of cowardice, infamy, and treason, punishable by death.
He understood that the very minute the option of a separate peace
was acted upon, even by a low-ranking officer commanding no
more than a company, the entire army ceased to exist. Either
everyone acts for the benefit of the entire army, or the "army" is an
anarchical mob, capable of great destruction, to be sure, but incapable of meaningful action.

The most effective leaders succeed in continually persuading
each member of the organization that only acts undertaken for
the collective benefit of the enterprise benefit them individually. This requires giving everyone a clear stake in the enterprise and the dual sense that they are indispensable to the
organization and the organization indispensable to them.

■

Lesson 151
The Art of Discipline

> "The conduct of a general in a conquered country is full of difficulties. If severe, he irritates and increases the number of his enemies. If lenient, he gives birth to expectations which only render the abuses and vexations inseparable from war the more intolerable. A victorious general must know how to employ severity, justness, and mildness by turns, if he would allay sedition or prevent it."
>
> ~Military Maxim LXX

The objective of a general in a conquered country is to "allay sedition or prevent it," nothing more and nothing less. This being the case, Napoleon recommended a course of conduct that walked a fine line between excessive severity on the one hand and excessive leniency on the other. Judgment and skill were required "to employ severity, justness, and mildness by turns."

Napoleon's recommendations for the policy of a general in a conquered country may be used to guide the policy of any manager faced with having to discipline or modify the behavior of a subordinate. As Napoleon identified for the general the objective of allaying or preventing sedition in the conquered country, so the manager must understand that his objective is to ensure that the subordinate understands his error or misconduct as well as what is required and expected in the future. The objective is to modify behavior, not punish or change a person. Accomplishing this requires a balance among something rather like Napoleon's "severity, justness, and mildness by turns." It demands uncompromising clarity and firmness in defining the desired result and explaining the consequences of failing to deliver the result, but it also calls for the expression of confidence and trust in the subordinate's ability to deliver what is required. Eliciting voluntary compliance is always preferable to compelling compliance by personal criticism, anger, or threat.

Lesson 152
Spin It

> "In establishing a hereditary nobility Napoleon had three aims,
> (1) to reconcile France with Europe, (2) to reconcile the old France
> with the new, (3) to wipe out in Europe the remnants of feudalism
> by associating the idea of nobility with that of public service and
> disassociating it from any feudal concept."
>
> ~Napoleon's third-person memorandum
> dictated at St. Helena after 1815

Ludwig van Beethoven, the story goes, having completed his Third
Symphony, the "Eroica," dedicated it to Napoleon Bonaparte, only
to tear the dedication page to shreds on hearing that he had proclaimed himself emperor. The new dedication read simply "To the
memory of a great man."

Beethoven's response was representative of the betrayal many
liberals felt after Napoleon, having brought a breath of reform and a
measure of democracy to peoples held in thrall to outworn empires,
created an empire of his own. For his part, Napoleon made no apol-
ogies, but he did seek to justify what he had done, and, in exile on
St. Helena, he even dictated a third-person memorandum explaining
his establishment of a new hereditary nobility as a rational and even
a revolutionary act. He claimed that the hereditary nobility was
necessary, in part, to reconcile France with the rest of Europe and to
reconcile pre-revolutionary with post-revolutionary France. His
third reason, however, is the most intriguing. He wrote that he had
effectively redefined the entire concept of hereditary nobility by
transforming it into a vehicle of public service rather than a product
of outworn feudalism.

Whether we find Napoleon's justifications convincing or not,
we are compelled to marvel at one of history's first recorded
attempts at "spin," the framing of an unpopular, dubious, or just
plain bad action in positive terms. In effect, Napoleon asked
posterity to believe that he had transformed the concept of nobility

into something truly noble—noble on account of policy, philosophy, and deed rather than by mere fiat of inherited title.

The art of spin is a most delicate one because the line separating spin from the truth is often broad and bright, whereas that separating spin from a lie is just as frequently thin and dim. If the truth were always simple and objective, there would be no excuse for spin. But much of what we do is complex. Truth may not only be difficult to understand, it is also rarely so objective as to be self-evident to all the stakeholders of an organization. For this reason, CEOs and managers must master the art of spin so they can exercise some control over the interpretation of the truth.

The generally acceptable and morally defensible goal of spin is to put actions, events, and policies in the best possible, most favorable light. Clearly, this is not the only light, but it is not the leader's responsibility to use the others. The truth will always be colored by perception. It is morally and intellectually unacceptable to manipulate, distort, or deny the truth, but influencing the perception of the truth is an important aspect of creating an optimal environment for your business. Doing so typically requires a persuasive exercise in explanation, redefinition, and what might be broadly called recontextualization—that is, presenting the facts in a context that might be new or unfamiliar. Napoleon's third justification for having created a hereditary nobility—to make nobility truly noble—is a virtuoso example of recontextualization.

■

6

Napoleonic Synergy

Lesson 153
Napoleonic Synergy 1

> "Infantry, cavalry, and artillery are nothing without each other;
> therefore they should always be so disposed in cantonments as to
> assist each other in case of surprise."
>
> ~ Military Maxim XLVII

The infantryman will tell you "infantry is the queen of battle." The cavalryman believes the cavalry is the most important branch of an army. And the artilleryman will cite Napoleon himself, who declared, "wars are won with artillery."

Rivalry among the combat arms is as old as the very notion of separate combat arms. Roman infantrymen must have argued with Roman charioteers. And until very recently, something similar was true in modern armies. Historians have often pointed to interservice rivalry and failure to communicate between army and navy commands as the main reasons why vital warnings failed to be communicated in the days and hours leading up to the "surprise" attack on Pearl Harbor on December 7, 1941. The creation of a U.S. Department of Defense in 1947 was largely an effort to end destructive rivalries and inefficiencies. At the time, some believed the goal of unifying the services was not only unrealistic, but undesirable because they deemed competition among the services to be both healthy and productive. Today, however, the "combined arms" approach is official doctrine. Any modern military operation of significant size and scope is conducted with marine, army, navy, and air force components closely coordinated and under tightly integrated combined command.

Call it "Napoleonic synergy."

His "Military Maxim XLVII" must have come as a radical statement in the early nineteenth century, when conventional commanders were accustomed to thinking of an army's combat arms as quite separate, certainly valuable in themselves, and the objects of legitimate arguments as to which was superior. To declare them "nothing without each other" was clearly a deliberate provocation on Napoleon's part, intended to shake up conventional thinking.

In practical field terms, Napoleon understood that the perpetual rivalry among the combat arms meant that generals tended to encamp artillery, cavalry, and infantry units in isolation from one another to prevent fistfights among the enlisted men and duels among the junior officers. Cavalrymen and infantrymen especially made sport of insulting one another, often to the point of drawing blood. Putting the different service arms in separate cantonments might make camp life more tranquil, but it also rendered the cantonments liable to enemy surprise attack. An encamped artillery unit, for example, was highly vulnerable to a hit-and-run cavalry raid, especially if no friendly cavalry or infantry units were nearby to assist. Similarly, an infantry attack against isolated cavalry and/or infantry units was most efficiently driven off by artillery.

Napoleon's top priority was fitness for victory in combat. All else—including tradition and traditional rivalries—came in a distant second.

> **If your enterprise** is not greater than the sum of its parts, your organization is not driven by "Napoleonic synergy." Lead so as to transform your enterprise from a collection of *me, me,* and *me* to a single *us* working toward objectives and goals that are neither *mine* nor *yours* but *ours*. Individuality of thought and imagination are valuable, but every employee must contribute to ends that are both universally understood and commonly valued.

■

Lesson 154
Napoleonic Synergy 2

> "The practice of mixing small bodies of infantry and cavalry together
> is a bad one, and attended with many inconveniences. The cavalry
> loses its power of action. It becomes fettered in all its movements. Its
> energy is destroyed; even the infantry itself is compromised, for on
> the first movement of the cavalry it is left without support."
>
> ~Military Maxim XLIX

Napoleon worked to achieve the true tactical integration of the combat arms, not their simple admixture. Combined indiscriminately, the branches could conflict with each other, canceling out the strengths specific to one or the other or both instead of augmenting them. Napoleon observed that mixing small bodies of cavalry and infantry together resulted in tying the fast-moving cavalry to the slower-moving foot soldiers, so that the cavalry "becomes fettered in all its movements. . . . Its energy . . . destroyed." For its part, the infantry also suffers. As soon as the cavalry detaches to move separately, the infantry is left unsupported.

Effective integration of combat arms requires that they be allowed to retain their separate identities and virtues. Their work should be directed toward common objectives, but they cannot be combined operationally in ways that ignore their specific strengths, vulnerabilities, limitations, and needs.

Creating synergy requires tactical and strategic coordination whereby the special strengths of each team or unit complement and support the other. The objective of Napoleonic synergy is to correct weaknesses and augment strengths. This cannot be achieved by simply piling one resource upon another. Teams or units working together must be able to do so without compromising, diluting, or surrendering their individual unique assets.

■

Lesson 155
Napoleonic Synergy 3

> "Charges of cavalry are equally useful at the beginning, the middle, and the end of a battle. They should be made always, if possible, on the flanks of the infantry, especially when the latter is engaged in front."
>
> ~ Military Maxim L

Napoleonic synergy seeks to make maximum use of all assets at all times. Traditional generals of the Napoleonic era used cavalry as shock troops to make the initial charges in a battle; sometimes, they also employed cavalry at the end of a battle to pursue a retreating enemy. (Napoleon observed this himself in his Military Maxim LI—see "Napoleonic Synergy 4" on the facing page.) Departing sharply from convention, Napoleon advocated a role for cavalry throughout the battle, provided that cavalry was used to augment the efforts of the other combat arms and not interfere with them. In the middle of a battle—during which most generals had little use for cavalry—Napoleon employed his mounted troops to attack the flanks of the enemy infantry while his own infantry concentrated on the enemy's front. This ensured a strongly synergistic attack in which both cavalry and infantry directed their efforts against the same enemy force, but from different directions, thereby avoiding any conflict with one another.

An asset is a liability whenever it is allowed to lie unused. Plan to keep all members of your organization in continually productive and genuinely synergistic engagement.

■

Lesson 156
Napoleonic Synergy 4

> "It is the business of cavalry to follow up the victory, and to pre-
> vent the beaten enemy from rallying."
>
> ~Military Maxim LI

In contrast to more conventional generals of his day, who used cavalry at the opening and closing of battle, Napoleon envisioned a role for this combat arm in all phases of battle, including the middle. He also assigned a specialized role to cavalry *after* battle. Whereas most commanders used it to round up enemy stragglers, Napoleon employed cavalry both more aggressively and more proactively. His objective was not to pick off the survivors of a battle, but to ensure a truly decisive victory by preventing "the beaten enemy from rallying" and thereby mounting a counterattack.

Napoleon sought to maximize the decisive outcome of battle, to ensure that the application of *tactics* produced the final *strategic* result he wanted. What is more, he never proposed mere destruction as the aim of combat. The role of cavalry was not to kill those left alive after the main fight, but to make sure the enemy could not re-form for a counterattack. He used cavalry to ensure that the decision of battle, which had been fought largely with infantry and artillery, was final. If combat was a sentence, cavalry was its period.

Strategy without tactics is nothing more than theory. Tactics without strategy is nothing more than a set of empty gestures. Napoleon never drew his sword without intending to use it purposefully.

A Napoleonic Chronology

1769

August 15: Born in Ajaccio, Corsica.

1779

May 17: Begins study at the royal military academy, Brienne-le-Château, France.

1784

October 17: Having graduated from Brienne, enrolls in the École Militaire, Paris.

1785

October 28: Graduates from École Militaire, having completed the two-year course in a single year; commissioned a second lieutenant in the artillery.

1785–89

Serves in garrisons in Valence, Drôme, Auxonne, and elsewhere.

1789

July 14: The French Revolution begins with the fall of the Bastille.

1789–91

September 16, 1789–February 13, 1791: Secures leave of absence from the French army and goes to Corsica, where he engages in revolutionary actions; returns to Paris on February 13, 1791, having overstayed his leave by months; absence excused.

1791

June 2–August 29: Serves with 4th Regiment of Artillery as first lieutenant.

August 30: Returns to Corsica.

1792–97: WAR OF THE FIRST COALITION
1792

April: Elected lieutenant colonel, 2d Battalion of Corsican Volunteers.

May 2: Leaves Corsica for France, where he has been dismissed from the French army for absence without leave.

June 20: Mob storms Tuileries Palace.

August 10: Tuileries is sacked, king's Swiss Guard is slaughtered, and Louis XVI is dethroned.

August 30: Reinstated and promoted to captain.

September 14: Returns again to Corsica to participate in revolutionary activity.

September 21: French Republic is proclaimed.

1793

January 21: Louis XVI is executed.

June 11: Having split with the nationalist leader Pasquale Paoli, Napoleon and the Buonaparte family flee Corsica for France.

October 9–December 19: Commands artillery at Siege of Toulon; promoted to major; plays key role in wresting Toulon from Royalist control.

December 22: In recognition of his brilliance at Toulon, provisionally promoted to brigadier general.

1794

August 9–20: Held under house arrest on suspicion of being a Jacobin supporter of Robespierre.

1795

October 5: Ends a Royalist attempt to storm the National Convention (13 Vendémiaire) with a "whiff of grapeshot."

October 15: Meets Josephine de Beauharnais.

October 20: With aid of Directory member Paul Barras, promoted to Commander of the Army of the Interior (commander of Paris military district).

1796

March 2: Assigned command of the French Army of Italy.

March 9: Marries Josephine.

March 11: Commences Italian campaign against Austria.

May 10: Wins Battle of Lodi.

November 17: Wins Battle of Arcola (Arcole Bridge).

1797

January 14: Wins Battle of Rivoli.

February 2: Austria surrenders Mantua.

April 18: Austria signs Treaty of Leoben.

October 17: Treaty of Campo Formio affirms and expands Treaty of Leoben, gaining France much territory.

December 5: Returns to Paris a hero.

1798-1802: WAR OF THE SECOND COALITION
1798
May 19: Begins Egyptian campaign.

July 2: Takes Alexandria.

July 21: Defeats Mamelukes at Battle of the Pyramids.

July 24: Takes Cairo.

August 1: Admiral Lord Nelson destroys the French fleet at Battle of Aboukir.

August 23: Leaves Egypt to return to France.

1799
November 9–10: Becomes First Consul in coup d'état of 18 Brumaire.

1800
February 19: Moves into the Tuileries Palace.

May 20: Leads army across the Alps to commence the second Italian campaign.

June 14: Defeats Austria at Battle of Marengo.

1801
February 9: Treaty of Luneville partitions Venice and gives France the left bank of the Rhine and the Austrian Netherlands.

July 15: Concordat between France and Rome restores Roman Catholicism to France.

1802
March 27: Treaty of Amiens signed with Britain.

May 1: Institutes sweeping reform of French educational system.

May 19: Establishes Legion of Honor.

August 4: New constitution names Napoleon First Consul for life.

1803–06: WAR OF THE THIRD COALITION
1803

March 5: Promulgates Civil Code ("Code Napoléon").

May 3: Louisiana Purchase concluded with United States.

May 16: Britain breaks Treaty of Amiens, re-igniting war.

1804

March 21: Napoleon orders execution of Duke of Enghien.

May 18: Senate proclaims Napoleon emperor.

December 2: Crowns himself and Empress Josephine at Notre
Dame Cathedral, Paris.

1805

March 17: Crowned king of Italy in Milan.

September 25: Crosses Rhine in Ulm campaign.

October 20: Wins Battle of Ulm, defeating Austrian forces poised
to invade France.

October 21: At Battle of Trafalgar, Nelson deals French fleet
another decisive defeat.

December 2: Wins Battle of Austerlitz against Austria and Russia.

December 26: Treaty of Pressburg further expands French Empire.

1806–07: WAR OF THE FOURTH COALITION
1806

February 15: Names his brother Joseph king of Naples.

June 5: Names his brother Louis king of Holland.

July 1: Forms Confederation of the Rhine with himself as its
"protector."

August 6: Presides over dissolution of Holy Roman Empire; Holy
Roman Emperor Francis II becomes Francis I of Austria and the
Confederation of the Rhine.

October 14: Wins Battles of Jena and Auerstadt.

October 27: Occupies Berlin.

1807

February 8: Bloody Battle of Eylau with Russians ends in draw.

June 14: Wins decisive Battle of Friedland.

July 7: Czar Alexander I signs Treaty of Tilsit, partitioning Prussia, ceding Polish provinces as the Duchy of Warsaw under Saxony, and ceding provinces on left bank of River Elbe, along with Hesse-Cassel, as Kingdom of Westphalia, to be ruled by Jérôme Bonaparte.

October 27: Concludes secret Treaty of Fontainebleau with Spain to partition Portugal, thereby beginning Peninsular War.

November 30: Napoleon's Marshal Junot enters Lisbon.

1808

February 20: Sends Marshal Joachim Murat to invade Spain under pretense of marching to reinforce occupation of Portugal.

May 2: Murat suppresses Spanish revolt against French occupation.

May 9: Charles IV of Spain abdicates.

June 4: Names brother Joseph king of Spain; Murat replaces him as king of Naples.

1809: WAR OF THE FIFTH COALITION
1809

April 20: Wins Battle of Abensberg.

April 22: Wins Battle of Echmuhl.

May 13: Occupies Vienna.

May 22: Defeated at Battle of Essling.

July 6: Decisively defeats Austrians at Battle of Wagram.

October 14: By Treaty of Schoenbrunn, Austria cedes more territory to the French Empire.

December 15: Divorces Josephine.

1810

April 2: Marries Austrian Archduchess Marie-Louise (she is eighteen, he is forty).

July 3: Louis Bonaparte abdicates Dutch throne.

July 9: Holland annexed to French Empire.

1811

March 20: Son born; referred to as the "King of Rome."

1812–14: WAR OF THE SIXTH COALITION
1812

June 24: Commences Russian campaign.

September 7: Defeats Russian army at Battle of Borodino.

September 14: Enters Moscow, which is abandoned and burning.

October 19: Commences long retreat through Russia, which devastates his army.

December 18: Arrives in Paris.

1813

May 2: Defeats Russians and Prussians at Battle of Lutzen.

May 20–21: Defeats Russians and Prussians at Battle of Bautzen.

June 21: Duke of Wellington decisively defeats Joseph in Spain at Battle of Vittoria.

August 10: Austria joins Allies to oppose France.

August 26–27: Defeats Allies at Battle of Dresden.

August 30: Napoleon's General Vandamme routed at Battle of Kulm.

October 16–19: Defeated at Battle of Leipzig, biggest battle of Napoleonic Wars.

October 30: Wins Battle of Hanau.

1814

January: Allies converge on France.

March 25: Allies advance on Paris.

March 28: Marie-Louise and Napoleon's court evacuate Paris.

March 30–31: Paris falls.

April 2: Senate proclaims end of French Empire.

April 4: Abdicates; Louis XVIII restored.

May 4: Exiled to Elba; wife and son take refuge in Vienna.

1815: WAR OF THE SEVENTH COALITION
1815

February 26: Escapes from Elba.

March 1: Lands near Cannes.

March 19: Louis XVIII flees Paris.

March 20: Enters Paris, beginning the "Hundred Days" of his new reign.

June 16: Wins battles of Ligny and Quatre Bras early in Waterloo campaign.

June 18: Definitively defeated at Battle of Waterloo.

June 22: Abdicates for second time.

July 15: Surrenders to Captain Frederick Maitland, Royal Navy, and demands political asylum.

August 8: Exiled to St. Helena.

October 15: Arrives at St. Helena.

1821

May 5: Dies, apparently of stomach cancer.

Further Reading

Asprey, Robert. *The Reign of Napoleon Bonaparte*. New York: Basic Books, 2001.

_____. *The Rise of Napoleon Bonaparte*. New York: Basic Books, 2000.

Barnett, Correlli. *Bonaparte*. New York: Hill and Wang, 1978.

Bergeron, Louise. *France under Napoleon*. Princeton: Princeton University Press, 1990.

Bertrand, Henri-Gratien. *Napoleon at St. Helena*. New York: Doubleday, 1952.

Blackburn, Julia. *The Emperor's Last Stand: A Journey to St. Helena*. New York: Vintage Books, 1993.

Bowden, Scott. *The Glory Years of 1805–1807: Napoleon and Austerlitz*. Chicago: The Emperor's Press, 1997.

Bruce, Evangeline. *Napoleon and Josephine: An Improbable Marriage*. London: Weidenfeld & Nicolson, 1995.

Cairnes, William E. *Napoleon's Military Maxims*. Mineola, NY: Dover, 2004.

Carrington, Dorothy. *Napoleon and His Parents*. New York: Dutton, 1990.

Chandler, David G. *Dictionary of the Napoleonic Wars*. London: Greenhill Books, 1979.

_____. *Napoleon*. New York: Saturday Review Press, 1973.

_____. *The Campaigns of Napoleon*. New York: Scribner, 1966.

_____. *Waterloo: The Hundred Days*. London: Osprey Publishing, 1980.

Connelly, Owen. *Historical Dictionary of Napoleonic France, 1799–1815*. Westport, CT: Greenwood Press, 1985.

_____. *The French Revolution and Napoleonic Era*. Fort Worth, TX: Holt, Rinehart and Winston, 1991.

Cornwell, Bernard. *Waterloo*. New York: Penguin, 1991.

Cronin, Vincent. *Napoleon Bonaparte: An Intimate Biography*. New York: William Morrow, 1972.

D'Aguilar, G. C., trans. *Napoleon's Art of War*. New York: Barnes & Noble Books, 1995.

Dallas, George. *Final Act: The Roads to Waterloo*. New York: Henry Holt & Company, 1997.

Elting, John R. *A Military History and Atlas of the Napoleonic Wars*. Mechanicsburg, PA: Stackpole Books, 1999.

_____. *Swords around a Throne: Napoleon's Grande Armée*. New York: DaCapo Press, 1997.

Englund, Steven. *Napoleon: A Political Life*. New York: Simon & Schuster, 2004.

Esdaile, Charles. *The Wars of Napoleon*. New York: Longman Group Limited, 1995.

Foreman, Laura. *Napoleon's Lost Fleet*. New York: Random House, 1999.

Gulland, Sandra. *The Many Lives and Secret Sorrows of Josephine B.* New York: Simon and Schuster, 1995.

Haythornthwaite, Philip. *Napoleon: The Final Verdict.* London: Arms and Armour, 1998.

Hofschroer, Peter. *1815: The Waterloo Campaign.* Mechanicsburg, PA: Stackpole Books, 1998.

Horne, Alistair. *How Far from Austerlitz: Napoleon 1805–1815.* New York: St. Martin's Press, 1996.

Kauffmann, Jean-Paul. *The Black Room at Longwood: Napoleon's Exile on Saint Helena.* New York: Four Walls Eight Windows, 1999.

Ludwig, Emil. *Napoleon.* New York: Boni and Liveright, 1926.

Luvaas, Jay, ed. *Napoleon on the Art of War.* New York: Touchstone, 1999.

Lyons, Martyn. *Napoleon Bonaparte and the Legacy of the French Revolution.* New York: St. Martin's Press, 1994.

Mansel, Philip. *The Eagle in Splendour: Napoleon I and His Court.* London: Philip Mansel, 1987.

Markham, Felix. *Napoleon.* New York: Penguin Books, 1963.

McLynn, Frank. *Napoleon: A Biography.* New York: Arcade Publishing, 2002.

Muir, Rory. *Britain and the Defeat of Napoleon 1807–1815.* New Haven: Yale University Press, 1996.

_____. *Tactics and the Experience of Battle in the Age of Napoleon.* New Haven: Yale University Press, 1998.

Phipps, R. W., ed. *Memoirs of Napoleon Bonaparte, Complete, by Louis Antoine Fauvelet de Bourrienne, His Private Secretary.* New York: Charles Scribner's Sons, 1891.

Riley, J. P. *Napoleon and the World War of 1813: Lessons in Coalition Warfighting.* London: Frank Cass Publishers, 2000.

Schom, Alan. *Napoleon Bonaparte.* New York: Harper Collins
Publishers, 1997.

Smith, Digby. *The Decline and Fall of Napoleon's Empire: How the
Emperor Self-Destructed.* London: Greenhill Books, 2005.

Thompson, J. M. *Napoleon's Letters.* London: Prion Books, 1998.

Weider, Ben, and Sten Forshufvud. *Assassination at St. Helena
Revisited.* New York: John Wiley and Sons, 1995.

Woloch, Isser. *Napoleon and His Collaborators: The Making of a
Dictatorship.* New York: W. W. Norton, 2001.

_____. *The New Regime: The Transformation of the French Civic Order
1789–1820.* New York: W. W. Norton and Company, 1994.

Lesson Index

[241]

Lesson 4

Do an Arcola 37

After watching several futile and costly assaults . . . Napoleon jumped from his horse, pulled together some troops by appealing to "the conquerors of Lodi bridge," wrapped a flag around a sword and started toward the [Bridge of Arcole].

Lesson 5

The Resolution to Conquer 38

In war tentative measures . . . lose everything.

Lesson 6

Believe Your Own Story 39

I am destined to change the face of the world; at any rate this is my belief.

Lesson 7

Serve 40

I fear insurrection caused by a shortage of bread—more than a battle against 200,000 men.

Lesson 8

Time Your Audacity 41

The art of being sometimes audacious and sometimes very prudent is the secret of success.

Lesson 9

Leadership Onstage 42

It is essential to display confidence.

Lesson 10

Enforce Ethical Standards 43

Every straggler who . . . detaches himself from his unit to maraud will be arrested, judged by a military commission, and executed within the hour.

a battle the enemy's loss is nearly equal to your own—whereas in a retreat the loss is on your side only.

Lesson 17

Safety in Courage 50

In a retreat, besides the honor of the army, the loss of life is often greater than in two battles. For this reason, we should never despair while brave men are to be found with their colors. It is by this means we obtain victory, and deserve to obtain it.

Lesson 18

If You Want to Be Victorious, Act Like a Winner 51

A general of ordinary talent occupying a bad position, and surprised by a superior force, seeks his safety in retreat; but a great captain supplies all deficiencies by his courage, and marches boldly to meet the attack. By this means he disconcerts his adversary; and if the latter shows any irresolution in his movements, a skillful leader, profiting by his indecision, may even hope for victory, or at least employ the day in maneuvering—at night he entrenches himself, or falls back to a better position. By this determined conduct he maintains the honor of his arms, the first essential to all military superiority.

Lesson 19

Be Aggressive in Preserving Your Options 52

When you are occupying a position which the enemy threatens to surround, collect all your force immediately, and menace him with an offensive movement. By this maneuver you will prevent him from detaching and annoying your flanks, in case you should judge it necessary to retire.

Lesson 20

To Protect Your Assets, Use Your Assets 53

Artillery should always be placed in the most advantageous positions, and as far in front of the line of cavalry and infantry as possible, without compromising the safety of the guns.

Field batteries should command the whole country round from the level of the platform. They should on no account be masked on the right and left, but have free range in every direction.

Lesson 35

Value Is a Matter of Common Sense 72

To make supernatural efforts to cross unapproachable mountains and then find oneself still in the middle of precipices, defiles, and boulders . . . is to act contrary to common sense and therefore is contrary to the spirit of the art of war.

Lesson 36

Finding a Reason for War 73

It could be advantageous for the [French] republic to make the conquest of Egypt pave the way for a glorious peace with England.

Lesson 37

Free, Don't Tie, Your Hands 74

A Constitution should be short—and obscure.

Lesson 38

Win in the Other Guy's Mind 75

In the Moravian campaign [of 1806] I understood that the Russians, having no general of the first rank, would believe that the French army would retreat upon Vienna. They had to make it a high priority to intercept this road, when in fact the retreat of the [French] army throughout the Moravian campaign had never been intended to be toward Vienna. This single circumstance distorted all of the enemy's calculations and inevitably contributed to those movements that led to his defeat.

Lesson 39

Leave Nothing to Chance 76

My habit is to leave nothing to chance.

Lesson 40

Think Small 77

I strongly recommend that you have the troops maneuver as much in small groups as in the school of the battalion, so that they are accustomed to deploy rapidly while those who come in ranks perform fire by files.

Lesson 41

The Self-Sustaining Enterprise 79

War must nourish war.

Lesson 42

Never Allow Assets to Become Liabilities 80

Prepare a plan. . . . War consists of unforeseen events.

Lesson 43

Establish Your Position 82

War is a profession of positions.

Lesson 44

Cover Your Rear 83

It is contrary to every principle . . . to defend the head of the convoy in preference to the rest of it. . . . The tail is the point of greatest need of protection, since the enemy always attacks here.

Lesson 45

The Place for Artillery 84

Never forget that in war all artillery must be with the army and not in the park.

Lesson 46

Strategy Begins with What You Have 85

Vauban has organized entire districts into intrenched camps covered by streams, inundations, fortified towns, and forests, but he never contended that fortified cities alone could close the frontier.

Lesson 47

Ideal Plan versus Real World 86

In forming the plan of a campaign, it is requisite to foresee everything the enemy may do, and to be prepared with the necessary means to counteract it. Plans of campaign may be modified, ad infinitum, according to circumstances—the genius of the general, the character of the troops, and the topography of the theater of action.

Lesson 48
Exercise Impulse Control 87
All wars should be governed by certain principles, for every war should have a definite object, and be conducted according to the rules of art. A war should only be undertaken with forces proportioned to the obstacles to be overcome.

Lesson 49
Don't Just Play the Game, Own It 88
Among mountains, a great number of positions are always to be found very strong in themselves, and . . . dangerous to attack. In mountain warfare, the assailant has always the disadvantage; even in offensive warfare in the open field, the great secret consists in defensive combats, and in obliging the enemy to attack.

Lesson 50
Do the Unexpected 89
The line of operation should not be abandoned; but it is one of the most skillful maneuvers in war, to know how to change it, when circumstances authorize or render this necessary. An army which changes skillfully its line of operation deceives the enemy, who becomes ignorant where to look for its rear, or upon what weak points it is assailable.

Lesson 51
Have a Reason for Everything You Do 90
It should be laid down as a principle, never to have intervals by which the enemy can penetrate between corps formed in order of battle, unless it be to draw him into a snare.

Lesson 52
To Fight or to Settle? 91
The keys of a fortress are well worth the retirement of the garrison, when it is resolved to yield only on those conditions. On this principle it is always wiser to grant an honorable capitulation to a garrison which has made a vigorous resistance, than to risk an assault.

Lesson 53

Command Undivided 91

Lesson 54

How to Evade Leadership 93

Lesson 55

Illusory Assets Are Real Liabilities 94

Lesson 56

The "Natural Principle" 95

Lesson 57

You Must Know Mathematics 96

3 KNOWLEDGE AND PREPARATION

prevent the enemy from passing between them with impunity. . . . [A]nd every precaution should be taken to prevent an attack upon them in detail.

the advanced posts should put him in possession of all the movements of the army, and the disposition and management of the great park [main position] of artillery should depend upon this information.

rapidity of movement; the want of artillery, by the nature of the maneuvers; and the inferiority in cavalry, by the choice of positions. In such circumstances the morale of the soldier does much.

Lesson 155

Napoleonic Synergy 3 226

Charges of cavalry are equally useful at the beginning, the middle, and the end of a battle. They should be made always, if possible, on the flanks of the infantry, especially when the latter is engaged in front.

Lesson 156

Napoleonic Synergy 4 227

It is the business of cavalry to follow up the victory, and to prevent the beaten enemy from rallying.

Index

Sterling Books by Alan Axelrod

Winston Churchill, CEO: 25 Lessons for Bold Business Leaders
Gandhi, CEO: 14 Principles to Guide & Inspire

Profiles in Audacity: Great Decisions and How They Were Made
Profiles in Folly: History's Worst Decisions and Why They Went Wrong

The Real History of the American Revolution: A New Look at the Past
The Real History of World War II: A New Look at the Past
The Real History of the Cold War: A New Look at the Past

Risk: Adversaries and Allies: Mastering Strategic Relationships
Risk: The Decision Matrix: Strategies That Win